LOGICAL PROPERTIES

Logical Properties

Identity, Existence, Predication, Necessity, Truth

COLIN McGINN

CLARENDON PRESS· OXFORD
2000

OXFORD
UNIVERSITY PRESS

Great Clarendon Street, Oxford OX2 6DP

Oxford University Press is a department of the University of Oxford.
It furthers the University's objective of excellence in research, scholarship,
and education by publishing worldwide in

Oxford New York

Athens Auckland Bangkok Bogotá Buenos Aires Calcutta
Cape Town Chennai Dar es Salaam Delhi Florence Hong Kong Istanbul
Karachi Kuala Lumpur Madrid Melbourne Mexico City Mumbai
Nairobi Paris São Paulo Shanghai Singapore Taipei Tokyo Toronto Warsaw

and associated companies in Berlin Ibadan

Oxford is a registered trade mark of Oxford University Press
in the UK and certain other countries

Published in the United States
by Oxford University Press Inc., New York

British Library Cataloguing in Publication Data
Data available

Library of Congress Cataloging in Publication Data
Data available

McGinn, Colin, 1950-
Logical properties : identity, existence, predication, necessity, truth / Colin McGinn.
p. cm.
Includes bibliographical references and index.
1. Logic. I. Title.
BC71 .M36 2000   160--dc21   00-056653

ISBN 0-19-924181-3 (alk. paper)

1 3 5 7 9 10 8 6 4 2

Typeset in Janson
by J&L Composition Ltd, Filey, North Yorkshire
Printed in Great Britain
on acid-free paper by
Biddles Ltd, *www.biddles.co.uk*

PREFACE

THE first philosophy course I ever taught was on truth, back in 1974. At that time I was primarily a philosopher of language and logic. In later years I became drawn to topics in the philosophy of mind, as well as metaphysics and epistemology. My interest in philosophical logic went into abeyance for a decade or so. The work in this book was begun about five years ago, though some of the ideas date back to the 1970s and 1980s. For some reason I started thinking seriously about these topics again, and I found that my thoughts on each of them shared some common themes. Thus, after many years of not working on philosophical logic, I decided to put together a short book on the subject.

It has been a pleasure to work on such abstruse, pure, and rigorous topics after spending so much time thinking about messy subjects like consciousness (not to mention evil, beauty of soul, etc.). In philosophical logic it is possible to achieve real results, develop sharp arguments, come to definite conclusions. It has also been a pleasure to write an avowedly specialist book, without having to worry about accessibility to a wider audience.

I have written this book as clearly and economically as I can. I have not burdened the text with detailed discussions of recent literature, preferring to maintain a smooth flow of argument; the footnotes address some of the relevant literature, as well as respond to possible objections.

Philosophical logic is perhaps a less thriving subject than it was in my student days. I think that this is in part because it became too formalistic and divorced from philosophical concerns. The reader will observe that there are very few formulas or symbols in this book, and I have strived constantly to keep the philosophical issues in mind; my aim has been to bring philosophy back into philo-sophical logic. What makes topics like existence and necessity so fascinating is the way they combine perplexing metaphysical con-cerns with issues of logical analysis and linguistics. I hope it is apparent in this book that I have steered clear of the kind of for-malistic fetishism and scholasticism that has characterized too much philosophical logic in recent years.

The general theme of the book is a kind of realist anti-naturalism about logical properties. My tendency is to take logical notions at face value, instead of trying to reduce them to some-thing else. As elsewhere in philosophy, I believe in respecting the appearances. One of my contentions is that the quantifier has been overrated as a tool of logical and linguistic analysis; another is that the urge to define the various logical notions dealt with here has not in general been a successful project. Logical properties are what they are and not some other thing.

The book is intended for readers with some sophistication in philosophical logic, but I think it could be used in an advanced undergraduate course if suitably supplemented with background reading.

I am grateful to E. J. Lowe and Andre Galois, who as referees for Oxford University Press gave me detailed comments on the penul-timate draft; many of the footnotes are responses to points they raised. I am also grateful to Stephen Neale, with whom I taught this material in a graduate seminar at Rutgers, as well as to the stu-dents who attended.

C.McG.

New York
March 2000

CONTENTS

I. IDENTITY

MY PURPOSE in this chapter is to formulate a cluster of claims about the nature of identity. I shall not enter into an elaborate defence of these claims, since they are generally uncontroversial and have been defended adequately by others. My aim is to articulate a position that will be useful for later discussions of other topics. In many ways identity is a paradigm for other logical notions, and it serves to focus thought in other areas to be as clear as possible about the concept of identity. My general theme will be the simplicity and primitiveness of the notion of identity, and its absolutely fundamental role in our thought.

My first thesis is that identity is *unitary*. Frege writes: 'Identity is a relation given to us in such a specific form that it is inconceivable that various forms of it should occur.'[1] I want to explain the import of this dictum and to spell out what we are committed to denying if we take the dictum seriously. So let us ask: What kind of property or relation is *not* unitary in the sense Frege intends? Take the property expressed by '*x* is blue' or the relation expressed by '*x* is more intelligent than *y*': these do admit of various forms—shades of blue, types of intelligence. Frege's thought is that identity does not in this way divide up into sub-varieties (one could not write a good book entitled *The Varieties of Identity*[2]). There is no equivocation or vagueness in the notion of identity, and it operates as a determinate property not a determinable one. It is, as Frege also said, that unique

---

[1] *Basic Laws of Arithmetic*, ii. 254; quoted in Peter Geach, *Logic Matters*, 238. Geach cites Frege in order to disagree with him, holding that identity is relative to a sortal count noun.

[2] In the way that Gareth Evans's *Varieties of Reference* emphasized the very different ways in which different types of terms refer (despite some common themes).

relation a thing has to itself and to no other thing—period.[3] Its logical properties are reflexivity, symmetry, and transitivity. It is simply the relation x has to y when x is nothing other than y, when there is no distinction between x and y, when x *is* y. And when we grasp the notion of identity we implicitly understand that it admits of no qualification or variation. That is the Fregean thesis.

In order to appreciate better what the Fregean thesis comes to, let us consider three ways in which it might be challenged, noting the errors of these challenges. First, it might be said that identity divides into two basic sub-types: numerical identity and qualitative identity. Numerical identity relates an object only to itself, while qualitative identity can relate numerically distinct objects that share some number of properties—objects that are merely exactly similar. Thus I am qualitatively identical to my twin, but not numerically identical to him. This distinction is allied to, indeed equivalent to, the distinction between type identity and token identity: two occurrences of the letter 'a' are type identical without being token identical—that is, they are similar enough to be declared qualitatively the same. Are there, then, two types of identity relation at work here? Well, there is obviously a distinction between similarity relations and the (numerical) identity relation, but it is confused to interpret this as implying that identity comes in two varieties. In fact, a statement of so-called qualitative identity is really a statement of numerical identity (that is, identity *tout court*) about the *properties* of the objects in question: it says in effect that the properties of x and y are (numerically) identical.[4] My properties (or many of them) are the same as those of my twin; the property the token 'a' has of being an instance of a certain letter

[3] See 'On Sense and Reference'.
[4] Of course, I am assuming here that different objects can share the same properties, i.e. that there are genuine universals. A trope theorist will need a different account of similarity between objects, since he will not be able to explain this in terms of the numerical identity of differently instantiated properties. But even for a trope theorist it should be clear that so-called qualitative identity is really just similarity and not another species of identity. It would be better to drop talk of 'numerical' and 'qualitative' identity altogether, speaking instead simply of identity and resemblance.

type is shared (*that* property) by this second 'a'. In the limit, if x and y share all their properties, then this amounts to the fact that every property x has is a property y also has: for any property F that x has there is a property G that y has such that F is identical to G. So-called qualitative identity is just numerical identity of qualities on the part of possibly distinct objects. Put another way, if you find that for any property F that x has there is an identical property G that y has, and vice versa, then x is qualitatively identical to y. Thus qualitative identity is analysable in terms of numerical identity. And similarly for type and token identity: to say that x and y are type identical is to say that there is a single type T that x and y both are, i.e. the type that x exemplifies is identical (numerically) to the type that y exemplifies. There are not two identity relations at play here but merely a unitary notion of identity relating distinct kinds of entity. It is not that 'identical' is an incomplete predicate until we are told whether it is to be preceded by the modifiers 'numeri-cally' or 'qualitatively'. When we use 'identical' to relate distinct objects we are simply saying that the objects have the same proper-ties or are of the same kind, where this latter is plainly an example of straightforward (numerical) identity. When I say that this dog is the same breed as that dog I am simply affirming the identity of their respective breeds, not introducing a new kind of identity relation over and above the old one—as it were, a special non-strict kind of identity that fails to obey Leibniz's law. It is not that we have to countenance a 'looser' brand of identity to be set beside the original article. All identity is strict identity—or rather, the qualifier 'strict' is pleonastic here.[5]

---

[5] I take it to be obvious enough that it would be a mistake to think that there are two modal kinds of identity, the necessary and the contingent. All identity is necessary, though there can be contingently true identity *statements*—those that contain non-rigid designators: see Saul Kripke, 'Identity and Necessity'. But even those who believe in contingent identity should not be tempted to construe this as a new type of identity relation, any more than the adjacency relation should be taken to have two forms or be 'incomplete' because numbers stand in necessary adjacency relations while chairs do not. It is the *same relation* that admits of the two modal qualifications. Compare the question of whether there are two kinds of truth property, corresponding to necessary truths and contingent truths.

A second reason for questioning Frege's dictum might be the alleged sortal relativity of statements of identity. The idea here is that to say that x is the same as y is not yet to express a complete proposition—we need to say what sort of sameness is in question. Until we answer the question 'same what?' we have said nothing truth-evaluable.[6] On this view, 'same' is radically syncategorematic, like 'er' in 'longer than'. A properly complete identity statement must have the form 'x is the same F as y', for some sortal F. This view certainly entails the denial of Frege's dictum, in either the view's strong form or its weak form. The strong form says that identity is relative, so that we can have instances in which x is the same F as y but not the same G. The weak form denies such relativity but insists that identity statements stand in need of sortal supplementation, where the various sortals generate distinct types of identity relation.[7] Thus 'same man' is not composed of a complete relation word 'same' that may stand alone between singular terms, combined with the common noun 'man'; rather, the noun is required to complete the sense of the incomplete symbol 'same'.

I would reject both the strong and weak versions of the sortal-dependence claim for familiar reasons. The strong relativity thesis conflicts with the indiscernibility of identicals, since if x is the same F as y but not the same G then x has a property y does not have, viz. being the same G as x. For if y has this property then it *is* the same G as x after all. Identity of x and y under the sortal F tells us, by Leibniz's law, that y must have what x has; but then if x has the property of being the same G as x, which it surely does, then y should have this property too—but this contradicts the claim that x

---

[6] As Geach puts it in 'Identity Theory': 'When one says "x is identical with y", this, I hold, is an incomplete expression; it is short for "x is the same A as y", where "A" represents some count noun understood from the context of utterance—or else, it is just a vague expression or a half-formed thought' (*Logic Matters*, 238).

[7] The strong position is defended by Geach, and the weak position sometimes seems intended by David Wiggins in *Sameness and Substance*, ch. 2.

is not the same G as y.[8] And once the thesis of relativity is abandoned the motivation for the incompleteness claim vanishes: any force there is in the claim that 'this is the same as that' is incomplete is better explained by the observation that the singular terms need supplementation in order to achieve determinate reference; once we know *which* object is at issue it is completely determinate whether this object is or is not identical to some other determinately specified object.[9] Unsupplemented identity statements are no more incomplete than 'x is blue', where also we can raise doubts about *which* thing is blue—as when I point in the direction of a mostly red car with a blue hood and say 'that is blue'. And really it is bizarre to think that identity could need supplementation in this way, since it is quite clear what relation is expressed by the simple sign of identity: if you put '=' between any pair of determinate singular terms the proposition expressed is as clear as a proposition could be.[10]

A third reason for denying that identity is unitary might issue from the recognition that objects come in many kinds and that the conditions of their persistence vary depending upon what kind of object is in question. Here we encounter the idea that objects have different 'criteria of identity', different conditions under which x may be said to be the same as y. Sets are the same iff they have all the same members; material objects are the same iff they are 'spatio-temporally continuous'; times are the same iff the same

---

[8] See Wiggins, *Sameness and Substance*, ch. 1, for this type of argument. Of course, the argument assumes the validity of the classical Leibnizian law, which a defender of relative identity might opt to reject. But I think that this law is so fundamental to the notion of identity that rejecting it amounts to changing the subject. I also believe, though I will not argue it here, that the thesis of relative identity enjoys no indispensable explanatory advantage over classical absolute identity; again, see Wiggins, ibid. 23 ff.

[9] See John Perry, 'The Same *F*', for a convincing defence of this line.

[10] It seems natural when someone says 'this is the same as that' to press the question '*same what?*'; but it is equally natural to respond '*what* is the same?' The bare demonstratives leave the proposition underspecified, but the fault lies with them and not with the identity concept. Compare baldly asserting 'this exists', where the indeterminacy clearly lies with the demonstrative and not with the concept of existence.

events happen at them; events are the same iff they have the same causes and effects; selves are the same iff they exhibit appropriate 'mental connectedness' or have the same bodies. But, however plausible this idea of varying 'criteria of identity' might be, it is confused to believe that it shows that the identity relation itself admits of such variation. Many different kinds of objects can be blue, too—solids, liquids, gases, rays of light, persons—but this does not show that blueness itself reflects the differences in these objects. Similarly, though many kinds of objects stand in the identity relation, it does not follow that this relation itself reflects or incorporates the kinds in question. We might indeed allow that identity can be supervenient on a variety of bases in objects, depending upon the kind of object in question, but this does not imply that what thus supervenes is not a unitary property.[11] It is the same with existence, which we shall discuss in the next chapter: many different kinds of object exist, and their existence 'consists in' different kinds of conditions, but it does not follow that 'exists' is equivocal or incomplete. Identity is always reflexive, symmetrical, and transitive, and always obeys the indiscernibility of identicals, despite the fact that it applies to many kinds of object. Identity is not a different relation when applied to concrete and abstract objects, say, despite the deep differences between these types of object. We just have the same old identity concept applied to a variety of objects, that is all.

I take it, then, that Frege's unitary thesis is not threatened by these kinds of consideration. Identity is such a specific relation, as specific (say) as the successor relation in arithmetic, that it is indeed inconceivable that it might fall into a variety of forms loosely classified together under 'same'. The concept of identity is quite unlike the family resemblance concept expressed by 'game',

---

[11] Compare the property of goodness: it supervenes on a variety of descriptive bases, but this does not compromise its conceptual integrity. Similarly, identity might be constituted by different things for different types of object, but it does not follow that identity itself shifts its identity from case to case (identity does not suffer from identity problems).

which is given to us in a highly unspecific form and admits of many subvarieties. Objects that fall under 'game' are not linked by a single common feature, but 'identical' expresses a quite definite concept that remains rigidly the same (!) from case to case.

The next question I want to ask is whether identity is definable: is its specificity the result of a sharp definition or is it conceptually primitive? In particular, can identity be defined by Leibniz's law, namely '$x = y$ iff for all P, Px iff Py'? There are three main problems with this proposal, which again I will simply summarize rather than defend. First, the sufficiency of the right-hand side notoriously depends upon whether we include identity-invoking properties in the range of the second-order variable: that is, do we include the property of being identical with x as one of the properties y has? If we don't, then the condition looks insufficient; if we do, then it involves a circle. It is certainly sufficient for x to be identical to y that x have the property of being identical to y! We don't want the definition to succeed only by embroiling it in such a gross circularity.

Second, and less familiar, the definition presupposes the notion of property identity. This is because we are saying precisely that x and y have the *same* properties: if x has all the same properties as y, then $x = y$. So we are using one application of identity to explain another application. We could, of course, go up a stage and try to define property identity by means of Leibniz's law: properties are identical iff they have all the same (second-order) properties. But this brings in the idea of identity again; and obviously the regress is vicious here. The point is even clearer if we formulate the definition in terms of parts or classes: $x = y$ iff x and y have all the same parts or belong to all the same classes. Here it is obvious that we are presupposing the idea of identity for parts and classes, so we cannot claim to be giving a general definition of identity. It might seem that the biconditional does not employ the notion of identity for properties or parts or classes, since it does not explicitly use the word 'same'; but the concept of identity is implicit in the use of variables, since we must assume that the same properties are assigned to the variables. In the same way, if we say 'for some x, x is F and x is G' we are making tacit appeal to the idea of identity in using 'x' twice here: it has to be the *same* object that is both F and G for this formula to come out true. In fact, this point about Leibniz's law just restates what we have already noticed about so-called qualitative identity, namely that it involves the numerical identity of properties. The case is really no different, in respect of circularity, from defining sameness of property by way of the condition that properties are the same iff they apply to the same objects: clearly this presupposes identity for the case of objects.

Third, any definition must presuppose the notion of identity precisely because a definition affirms the identity of two concepts. What Leibniz's law says, construed as a definition, is that the concept of identity is the *same* concept as the concept of indiscernibility. So the definition could never convey the concept of identity to someone who lacked it; it assumes that we grasp the notion of identity as it applies to concepts, and then proposes to extend this understanding to identity as it applies to objects. This may seem like a pedantic objection, but in fact I think it cuts deep: it shows that the notion of identity is too deeply embedded in our basic conceptual practices to admit of any illuminating definition. The very idea of definition itself presupposes it. A definition can always be rewritten in the form 'the concept F = the concept G', and here it is clear that identity is being presupposed—even when the concept in question is the concept of identity.[12]

Oddly enough, Frege himself affirms that Leibniz's law defines identity, saying: 'Now Leibniz's definition is as follows: "Things are the same as each other, of which one can be substituted for the

---

[12] I am being strict about definability here, and there are looser notions of definition that would not be subject to the circularity I am alleging. But my essential point is that the concept of definition as sameness of sense between definiendum and definiens itself contains the notion of identity—which is not the case for the vast majority of concepts we might hope to define. Truth, meaning, and identity are implicated in the notion of definition; but the same could not be said for the concepts of redness or justice or pain.

other without loss of truth". This I propose to adopt as my own definition of identity.[13] Perhaps he fails to notice the circularity in this because of the substitutional formulation he borrows from Leibniz, but this becomes apparent once we observe that the principle has to mean substitutivity in the *same* contexts (compare sharing the same properties)—not to mention the other two points I have made. It is, of course, true that identity obeys Leibniz's principle of the indiscernibility of identicals; but this is a far cry from the claim that the principle provides a non-circular definition of identity.

Let me also note the oddity of supposing that a singular statement should be analysable by means of a universally quantified statement. If I say that Hesperus is identical to Phosphorus, I seem to be making a singular relational statement about a given object, logically on a par with (say) 'Hesperus is brighter than Phosphorus'. But according to the Leibnizian definition I am doing no such thing: I am quantifying second-order-wise over properties and making a statement of generality. The two-place relation word turns into a quantifier and a biconditional—hardly what the surface grammar would suggest. On this view, identity statements are not really relational statements after all; in logical grammar they express a higher-order condition on properties, and are replaceable by quantified statements that do not have a relational form at all.

The upshot is that identity is not only unitary, it is also indefinable (assuming that Leibniz's law is the only plausible attempt to define identity). Identity is a primitive concept, and a concept that exists in only one form.

When a concept is primitive it is apt to be basic relative to other concepts. What I want to suggest now is that identity has a universality and basicness that is hard to overstate; concepts don't get more basic than this—or more indispensable. Every object (or any

[13] *Foundations of Arithmetic*, 76.

other entity—property, function, you name it) is self-identical; identity is not a relation an entity can fail to stand in to something. The concrete, the mental, the abstract—all instantiate the univocal concept of identity. In this respect, as in others, identity resembles existence; but it is even more universal than existence, since it holds even of non-existent objects. Sherlock Holmes does not exist, but he is self-identical; he is certainly not identical to Dr Watson, who enjoys his own identity relation to himself.[14] Even if these fictional entities are impossible objects they are still self-identical. Identity is a very undemanding relation; it holds even of objects that are purely intentional, not even denizens of some possible world. This is presumably one of the reasons it is typically counted a logical notion—its extreme generality. 'No entity without identity', Quine says; we might add, 'Identity with or without (existent) entity'. Whenever we have a subject of predication—existent, merely possible, non-existent—we have an application of the concept of identity to that subject. Identity is ontologically generous.

Second, the notions of identity and distinctness are given in the very idea of predication. When we predicate a property F of an object x two types of multiplicity are involved: that it is x and not some other object y that we are saying is F, and that F is but one of many properties that might be predicated of x. We are singling x out from a multiplicity of possible subjects of predication, and we are selecting F from among a range of properties that might be ascribed to x. So we have the thought of a plurality of at least possible objects that might or might not be F, and we have the thought that x may instantiate a range of other properties while not instantiating all other properties. But both these thoughts involve the idea of identity, since they bring in the idea of objects and properties that are *not* identical to x and F. The embedded notion of plurality is defined in terms of the notion of identity. The very idea of

---

[14] I am here assuming that non-existent objects can have properties, such as being a detective and being self-identical. This assumption will loom large in the next chapter.

the extension of a predicate incorporates the identity concept. So even to venture the thought that some object is some way is to introduce the twin ideas of identity and distinctness. And if predication is the most basic structure of thought, then identity is right there at the foundations.

Third, the logical law of identity has some claim to be basic among the traditional logical laws. The law of identity is banality itself: 'everything is identical to itself', or 'for all x, $x = x$'. Now consider the law of non-contradiction: 'nothing can be both F and not F'. What this says is that no *single* object can have a property and its contradictory. Of course *distinct* objects could be both F and not-F, since one could be F and the other be not-F. What is logically impossible is that one object should have contradictory properties. But to formulate this thought we need the concept of identity: the *same* object cannot be both F and not-F. In other words, if ever we have a case in which x is F and y is not-F then we can deduce that x is not identical to y; negating a property that x has always takes us to *another* object, not identical to the first. Understanding the way negation works here involves grasping the role of the concept of identity in fixing this law. The law of excluded middle works similarly. This law says that everything is either F or it is not-F. Take any object, you will find that it either has some property or it lacks that property; there is nothing in between. But this involves a cross-reference that signals a use of the notion of identity: x is either F or x (the *same* thing) is not-F. The thought is not that either x is F or some *other* object is not-F; it is that either x is F or it—that very object—is not-F. But this cross-reference involves the thought that we are dealing with an identical object at the two occurrences of the variable or pronoun. In other words, the apparatus of variable-binding, or pronominal anaphora, invokes the notion of identity.[15] This is equally true, of course, of the law of identity itself, so that the concept of identity is needed

---

[15] I cannot recall now where I first encountered this point about variables and identity, but I think it is generally appreciated.

to understand it also. My point is that we need this law to under-stand the other two laws; and if anyone failed to see that identity obeys the classical law then that would be a reason to doubt that they knew what they were talking about. Maybe it could also be argued that we need the other two laws in order to understand the law of identity, in which case we should rest with the weaker con-clusion that identity is presupposed in the other laws—and not the stronger claim that it is *more* basic than those laws. In any case, the law of identity will be presupposed in the other two laws: without a grasp of the law of identity the other two laws are not even so much as intelligible.

The very ubiquity and indispensability of identity has some-times worked as an incitement to declare it a pseudo-relation. Thus Wittgenstein wrote in the *Tractatus*: 'It is self-evident that identity is not a relation between objects' (5.5301); and 'Roughly speaking, to say of *two* things that they are identical is nonsense, and to say of *one* thing that it is identical with itself is to say noth-ing at all' (5.5303). He goes on to refer to standard identity sen-tences as 'pseudo-propositions' (5.534), stipulating a notation in which they cannot even be formulated; he prefers to express identity by sameness of sign, not by a special sign for the identity relation (5.53). The feeling that identity is a pseudo-relation is doubtless connected to the apparent triviality of the relation: it comes too cheaply, being found in every object whatsoever. It is therefore felt to be a redundant concept, a mere flourish. But consider the concept of distinctness, which is defined simply as the negation of identity. We might characterize distinctness, parodying Frege, as 'that relation which any object has to every object except itself'. Does this relation have the look of a pseudo-relation? Well, certainly not because it only relates an object to itself! On the contrary, it relates an object to a vast range of other objects. Surely it is clear that distinctness is a genuine relation between things; but then identity must also be, since it is simply the negation of distinctness. Negation cannot take us from a genuine relation to a pseudo-relation.

Both relations are important simply because we don't always *know* the truth about distinctness and identity; and it can be a matter of great moment whether or not it is the same or distinct things that are both *F* and *G* (e.g. whether two crimes were committed by a single person). If we were omniscient about identity, then indeed identity truths would not inform us of anything; but the same could be said of *any* kind of truth. Identity propositions are not always analytic or a priori, as Frege long ago taught us, so there is nothing trivial about such propositions. The claim of redundancy ignores the epistemic role that the concept of identity plays. (We shall encounter more such redundancy claims in later chapters.)

But what kind of relation is identity, metaphysically speaking? This is one of those loaded philosophical questions of which the ontologically anxious are so fond. Is it physical or mental? Is it causal or functional? Is it spatial or non-spatial? Where does it fit into our preferred set of allowable categories? Clearly, the answer is that it is none of the above. It is, for want of a better word, a *logical* relation. It is not a perceptible relation, since there is no sense-impression of self-identity. Nor is it a relation that generates causal powers—unlike, say, 'being of greater electrical charge than'. We might say that it is an abstract relation, if we insist on trying to categorize it; but then we must remember that it holds of concrete objects and that 'abstract' is little more than a label reserved for what is agreed to be neither mental nor physical. We shall be encountering several more such logical properties as we proceed, and I shall have more to say about their metaphysical status *pari passu*. For now, we can simply conform with tradition in classifying identity as a logical relation. And let us note that it is the only relation that is counted as a logical constant. All the other standard logical constants—the connectives and quantifiers—are operators on closed and open sentences. This makes '=' semantically quite unlike the other logical constants. The reason for so counting it is, presumably, that identity is the only relation that has a claim to topic-neutrality, which is to say universality:

identity holds of every entity in every possible world, and is part of our very framework of thought.[16]

I have endorsed four main theses about identity: (i) it is unitary, (ii) it is indefinable, (iii) it is fundamental, (iv) it is a genuine relation. I do not suppose that any of this is very controversial, putting aside some details of the ways I have chosen to state these theses. My aim has been to set out a general conception that will be useful later when we approach more difficult and controversial topics. This is the first instalment in a series of studies of what we might call logical ontology—the ontological character and standing of certain (broadly) logical notions. I shall be defending views of our other topics that mirror what I have said here about identity.

---

[16] Identity is also bound up with the apparatus of quantification, since variables are interpreted by means of it, as I noted earlier.

2. EXISTENCE

CONSIDER these sentences: 'Bill Clinton exists', 'Superman does not exist', 'Vulcan exists', 'Hillary Clinton does not exist'—the first two true, the second two false. It is extremely natural, going by surface syntax, to interpret these sentences as simple predications, having the same logical form as 'Bill Clinton runs', 'Superman does not drink', 'Vulcan spins', 'Hillary Clinton does not breathe'. Putting it in the material mode, it is natural to regard existence as a property that things may have or fail to have. Of course, this formulation is only as clear as the notion of a property, which is not altogether clear. About the best that can be said to define the relevant notion of property is that a property is something that objects have or instantiate. But if we ask what an object is we are soon driven back to the idea that an object is what has or instantiates properties.[1] The two notions are woven inextricably together. We should certainly not adopt some tendentious criterion, such as the idea that a property is what, when instantiated, makes a causal difference to how the world works, or be perceptible, or not be instantiated by everything that exists. Nor is it any help to fall back on the grammatical form of sentences, as when we say that a property is what a predicate expresses. Aside from being dubious in itself, this presupposes the notion of a predicate, which threatens to be defined as a term that expresses a property. Perhaps all we need to say, for present purposes, is that a property, in the intended sense, is what is instantiated by an object in a way analogous to the

---

[1] Additionally, we cannot informatively characterize the notion of property by using the notion of instantiation, since that notion is itself parasitic on the notion of property.

way in which (say) redness is instantiated by an object: that is, choose a paradigm property and declare a property to be anything that resembles this paradigm.[2] In any case, the traditional opposition to the idea that existence is a property has not relied upon the charge that the whole notion of a property is too unclear to make the claim well-formulated, or that the notion is being stretched too far when made to include existence. Indeed, it has typically been assumed that the claim is clear enough to be known to be demonstrably false: we know what it means to call existence a property; it is just that it is no such thing. Existence is nothing like redness or maleness or evenness, according to one tradition. But this, as I say, is not how statements of existence naively appear.

Assuming, then, that we have an adequate grip on the notion of property, and allied notions, we find it natural to talk in the following way. Not everything that we refer to exists: Venus does, Vulcan doesn't; horses do, unicorns don't. There are merely fictional entities as well as things that really exist. To exist is to have a property that only some of the things we refer to have—those that exist as opposed to those that are merely fictional. Thus existence is a property that is universal to entities that exist, unlike (say) the property of being blue (which is, however, universal to entities that are blue[3]). This universality is shared by certain other properties—such as self-identity and logical properties like not being blue and not blue at the same time. But despite the universality of the property of existence over existent things, the word 'exists' still does important distinguishing work, since not everything we talk about exists. Since there are objects of reference that don't exist, it is useful to have a word that ascribes the property of existence to a subset of what we refer to. This word has the logical role of a

---

[2] This is surely how the debate about whether existence is a property has been traditionally conceived: the question has always been whether 'exists' belongs with paradigm property terms like 'red' or 'fast' or 'prime'.

[3] In fact, there is no very clear sense in which existence is more universal than blueness: every blue thing is blue, as every existing thing exists; some existing things are not blue, as some blue things do not exist. *More* things exist than are blue, perhaps—but that is all.

predicate in statements of existence, so that 'Venus exists' and 'Venus spins' have the same logical form: they are both singular sentences involving a proper name and a property-ascribing predicate. Just as we say of Venus that it spins, so we say of it that it exists. The ontological status of existence as a property of objects has its semantic counterpart in the grammar of statements of existence: 'exists' is a predicate. It is a predicate that singles out the existent entities we talk about from those that are merely 'intentional'—fictitious, wrongly reified, hallucinatory, dreamed up, mistakenly posited. This sounds like a mere articulation of the common-sense view of existence, but of course it has been widely rejected, and its very coherence has been doubted. In this chapter I shall defend the naive view against the main rival position. The rival position, I shall argue, has severe and unfixable problems, while the naive view remains unthreatened. Let me first lay out the rival view as clearly as possible, before arguing against it.

It is extremely important to state as clearly as possible what it is that the orthodox rival view maintains, so that we fix in our minds exactly what the doctrine is. It is only too easy to miss the import of the doctrine in a formalistic haze. The thesis is that when you say that Bill Clinton exists you do not attribute to a certain *object* the property of existence, since there is no such property; what you do is say that some *property* is instantiated—where this property is not the property of existence itself but some other property to which you are alluding. Instead of attributing a property to an object you attribute a property to a property—the second-order property of having an instance. When you think of an object as existing what you are really thinking is that some property has an instance. You may try your hardest to focus on Clinton himself and ascribe to him the property of existence, but you cannot succeed in that endeavour, since the thought in question must always be to the effect that a certain property has an instance—as it might be, the property of being a US president who was once governor of Arkansas. It cannot be that two conceptual ingredients make up your singular existential thought—the concept of Clinton and the concept of existence; rather, there must be a third ingredient, corresponding to the property to which instances are ascribed. When you think that Clinton is male you can make do with just the two ingredients, but when you attribute existence to him you are driven to introduce some further property that Clinton has. Your thought is thus really about that property, not about Clinton, though it may seem otherwise to you.[4] The same goes for general existential thoughts: when you think that tigers exist you do not think of certain feline objects that each has the property of existence; rather, you think, of the property of tigerhood, that it has instances—no mental act of predicating existence of any object takes place. The orthodox doctrine gives the very analysis of the content of your thought—what the concept of existence intrinsically involves. The concept of an object existing simply is the concept of a property having instances. To think that Clinton exists is to think that the property of being a US president who was once governor of Arkansas has an instance.

Russell is the main architect of the orthodox view, or at least its most unflinching proponent. He fully grasped exactly what the doctrine says about what he would call the structure of an existential fact; he wasn't simply offering a notational reformulation of ordinary existential sentences. His clearest statement of the view runs as follows:

When you take any propositional function and assert of it that it is possible, that it is sometimes true, that gives you the fundamental meaning of 'existence'. . . . Existence is essentially a property of a propositional func-

---

[4] Imagine checking off a list of assertions about Bill Clinton, to the effect that he is president, that he smiles a lot, that he is intelligent, that he is imprudent, that he exists. For the first four items your thought is a subject–predicate thought about a certain concrete entity, but when it comes to the fifth item your thinking suddenly goes second-order as you mentally invoke some suitable propositional function to pin your existential thought upon. But doesn't it *seem* that you engage in the same kind of singular predication for the fifth case as for the first four? What, one wants to ask, is to *stop* you thinking singularly about Clinton when you essay an existential thought about him?

tion. It means that the propositional function is true in at least one instance. . . . We have got to have some idea that we do not define, and one takes the idea of 'always true', or of 'sometimes true', as one's undefined idea in this matter. . . . It will be out of this notion of *sometimes*, which is the same as the notion of *possible*, that we get the notion of existence. To say that unicorns exist is simply to say that '(x is a unicorn) is possible'.[5]

Russell goes on to compare 'exists' with 'numerous', saying that neither can be meaningfully predicated of individuals; we can only attach 'numerous' to a term expressing a propositional function, as in 'dogs are numerous'. He says: 'Exactly the same applies to existence, that is to say that the actual things that there are in the world do not exist, or, at least, that is putting it too strongly, because this is to utter nonsense.' The correct thing to say is that 'it is of propositional functions that you can assert or deny existence.'[6] It is a logical category mistake to ascribe existence to objects.

We can divide Russell's position here into three sub-theses: an ontological thesis, a semantic or logical thesis, and a definitional thesis. The ontological thesis has a negative and a positive part. Negatively, the claim is that existence is not a property that individuals instantiate. Positively, the claim is that for something to exist is for some property (propositional function) to have instances. In the metalinguistic terms Russell prefers, existence consists in a predicate yielding a truth under certain substitutions into its argument-place: there are true sentences containing that predicate and a substituted name. For example, 'tigers exist' means 'there are true sentences of the form "*a* is a tiger"', where '*a*' is a name of some tiger. So to say that an individual exists always involves a reference to some property or predicate of which it is said that it holds of something. Thus we have the semantic thesis

---

[5] 'The Philosophy of Logical Atomism', 232–3.

[6] Ibid. 233. Actually, this is a misformulation on Russell's part: it is not that you can *predicate* existence of propositional functions; rather, all statements of existence are equivalent to statements saying of propositional functions that they have instances. Propositional functions have the property of having instances, not the property of existence (there is no such property, for Russell).

that statements of existence are really higher-order statements involving reference to a property or concept or predicate or propositional function. The subject of the statement is never a term for an individual but always a term for a property, with the notion of existence being carried by a predicate that attaches to that other predicate term. Statements of existence are always and necessarily second-order statements, analogous to 'blue is delightful to the eye'. And now the definitional thesis is that 'exists' can be defined in these terms: when 'exists' occurs in a statement it can always be paraphrased in terms of the notions of a propositional function and being 'sometimes true' or 'possible'. Presumably Russell intends this definition to be non-circular, so that we are not compelled to explain the definiens by recourse to the definiendum; as he says, we 'get the notion of existence' out of these other notions. The notion of existence gets swallowed up into these other notions, no longer to masquerade as a predicate of individuals. In a perfect language the word need never occur, its job always being done by 'sometimes true' and its adjuncts.

Nowadays this Russellian position is routinely put by saying that existence is what is expressed by the existential quantifier and only by it. All natural language sentences that speak of existence can be translated into sentences that employ only the existential quantifier, with no use of 'exists' as predicative. The existential quantifier is conceived, following Frege, as a function from first-order concepts to truth-values, so that nothing corresponding to a first-order predicate is involved in its semantics.[7] So the assumption is that the Russellian conception of existence receives its canonical formulation in the thesis that 'exists' always means 'there is an x such that'. The thesis is that we can always translate existential statements into this form of words. This is how a perfect language expresses the idea that existence consists in a property having instances.

---

[7] For the Fregean view of quantification as a second-level function see Michael Dummett, *Frege: Philosophy of Language*, ch. 3.

I take it all this is familiar enough, even to the point of tedium. But I think that almost none of it is right: the Russellian thesis and its customary Fregean formulation are riddled with problems.

I shall consider four kinds of objection to the orthodox view. First, let us enquire into the innocent-seeming phrase 'has instances'. What does it mean? It can be taken in an objectual or a substitutional sense. In the objectual sense, the doctrine is that for something to exist is for there to be objects that are instances of some suitable predicate. Here are some objects, and they are instances of *F*. But that can only mean that these objects *exist*, so that we are saying that there exist instances of *F*, for some *F*. If they did not exist, then the existential statement would not be true after all. But how is that use of 'exists' to be analysed? Clearly it will be no help to say that they are instances of 'instances of *F*', since these will again need to be existent instances. The notion of existence is presupposed in the analysis, so the analysis does not settle what kind of notion it is. It might even be a predicate as it occurs in that use: for there to be instances of *F* is for there to be objects that exist, predicatively, and are instances of *F*. The instances have to be existent objects, so we are presupposing the notion of an existent object in our account of what an instance of a predicate is. We can put the objection this way: Consider 'planets exist' and ask whether Vulcan is an instance of 'planet'. If it is, then we have not correctly analysed existence, since Vulcan doesn't exist, and hence its planetary instancehood doesn't show that planets exist. But if it is not, then that can only be because it doesn't exist—thus demonstrating that the relevant notion of instance must import the concept of existence. If we say that 'planets exist' is true because 'Mars is a planet' is true and 'Vulcan is a planet' is not, that can only be because 'Mars' refers to an existent object while 'Vulcan' does not. The reason we get a truth in the one case and not the other is precisely that existence is ascribed to the reference of one term and not to the other. Why else would the one be true and the other not be? Nor will it help to introduce a distinction between fictional truth or fictional instance and literal truth or literal instance in order to rule out this kind of case, since this also presupposes the notion of existence. The point is that paraphrasing existence statements into statements about the instantiation of a property does not establish that existence is not a predicate, since the notion of instantiation must be taken to have existence built into it—it must be *existent* things that instantiate the property. It is this circularity that prevents the orthodox view from claiming to have established that existence is not a predicate.

I think Russell was at least subliminally aware of this problem, which is why he tended to formulate the doctrine in more substitutional terms. He preferred to say that there are true singular propositions or sentences that are instances of the propositional function in question, rather than say that there are instancing *objects* that satisfy that function. And what he liked best of all was the formulation in terms of possibility—'(x is a dog) is possible'—because that put him as far as possible away (he thought) from the concept of existence. It makes it look as if we are analysing—noncircularly analysing—the notion of existence in terms of modal notions and propositional functions. But this does not really help with the underlying problem. In the first place, it is necessary to assert the existence of certain propositions or sentences on this analysis, and the question must arise as to what this is supposed to amount to. It had better not mean that certain propositions or sentences have the property of existence.[8] But, more obviously, there is the problem of how to analyse the singular propositions themselves: what are their truth conditions? Clearly we cannot allow 'Vulcan is a planet' to be a substitution instance corresponding to 'planets exist', but that can only be because the referent of 'Vulcan' does not exist. For a singular statement to be true in the sense needed is for there to *be* an object referred to by the singular term and for that object to satisfy the attached predicate. So, again, the

---

[8] I return to this later when I discuss what it means to ascribe existence to properties or propositional functions.

notion of existence is smuggled in unanalysed. It is perfectly consistent with the higher-order paraphrase that existence is actually a property of objects: we can paraphrase existential statements that way if we like, but we are tacitly assuming that existence is a property of objects, for all that the paraphrase tells us. What is really being said, according to the paraphrase, is that among the objects that have the property of existing at least one of them is *F*—hence *F* has instances. Of course, this does not yet prove that 'exists' *is* a predicate—though it might incline us to think that—but it does show that the orthodox view has not refuted that doctrine, or made it redundant, simply by providing a plausible-sounding paraphrase in terms of properties and their instances. For the question precisely is what it *is* for a property to have instances—if not for objects that exist to instantiate the property.

We must here guard against adopting a formalistic approach to the issue. Russell did not make this mistake, but those in the tradition he initiated (with others) have tended to think that the issue could be settled simply by seeing whether existence statements could be translated into statements employing the so-called existential quantifier. But that cannot be right, because it is possible to interpret the quantifier by using a predicate of existence, along the lines of 'for some *x*, *x* exists and *x* is *F*' (I will come back to this). The question is whether the fundamental notion of existence can be explained in such a way as to avoid predicating it of objects, and merely giving a quantificational paraphrase does not show this, since it depends upon how the terms in the paraphrase are to be interpreted. The question can only be settled by direct philosophical argument, not by offering some purely formal translation of existence statements. We need to know whether the concept of existence contained in the symbol for the existential quantifier is or is not the first-order concept of predicative existence.[9]

---

[9] It is perfectly consistent to hold that '∃*x*' is a second-level expression, so that it forms sentences from first-level expressions, and that '∃*x*' abbreviates a condition containing a first-level concept of existence—as is evident from the conjunctive paraphrase of '∃*x*' that I suggest in the text and to which I will return.

The second problem has more of the character of a proof that the orthodox view cannot be a general analysis of the notion of existence, and not just a challenge to the adequacy of the account. Consider the existence of properties or propositional functions or predicates themselves. These exist in the same sense that other things exist, despite their being (presumably) abstract and non-individual. Thus we can say, 'the property of being a planet exists'—as we might if insisting (rightly or wrongly) upon the truth of realism as opposed to nominalism about universals. But how might this statement be analysed? On the orthodox view, we must make reference to some property that the entity said to exist is an instance of. It plainly cannot be the property of being a planet, since the property of being a planet isn't itself a planet. But what else could it be? We might try finding some true description of the property and inserting that into the analysis—say, the property of being currently under discussion; then for the property of being a planet to exist is for *that* property to have instances. But the difficulties now are obvious. First, there is the problem of securing uniqueness. But second, and worse, we are now launched on a vicious infinite regress, since we must ask what the existence of the higher-order property consists in, thus requiring a further property to be a property *of* that property.[10] The problem, evidently, is that to analyse the existence of a property we need another property that the first one instantiates, and so on *ad infinitum*. Not only is it doubtful that there always *are* these further properties, but also we will not succeed in getting any of them to exist without the existence of further ones that raise the same question. Intuitively,

---

[10] We don't avoid this regress by invoking the property of being identical to a certain property and then using this as the needed propositional function. That is, suppose we want to know what it is for property P to exist, and we suggest that it is for the propositional function '$= P$' to have an instance. This still refers to P, of course, but it jumps up a level by forming the higher-level function '$= P$', so that when we ask what it is for the referent of '$= P$' to exist we will need a function that expresses identity with that higher-order property—to wit, the property of being identical to the property of being identical with P. And so on up. Invoking identity in this way does not work to confine the generated properties merely to the property P we started out with.

the existence of a property is intrinsic to it; it is not a matter of some *relation* that the property stands in to some other property of which it is an instance. And if we construe it as such a relation, then we generate a vicious regress, as each new property raises the question of its own existence.[11]

Matters look less troublesome when we are considering the existence of individuals, since they always have properties to instantiate, and their existence doesn't require the existence of other individuals; but with properties themselves we find that we have to postulate extra properties for them to fall under, and we are then being faced with the question of *their* existence. No property will be able to exist unless a whole infinite series exists. But there is no such series, and anyway it would never get off the ground because of the regress. In effect, the orthodox view makes it impossible to attribute existence to properties; this would have to be declared ill-formed and meaningless (not merely false). And it is noteworthy that Russell never attempts to extend the analysis to this area of existence. One suspects that he (and others) simply take the existence of properties for granted, as if it needs no analysis. But this is no better than defending the thesis that existence is to be analysed as occupancy of space simply by declining to consider the existence of abstract entities like numbers. Any good theory of existence needs to be able to handle the full range of uses of 'exists'. In fact, this difficulty about property existence acts back on the analysis of individual existence, since the property the individual instantiates must itself exist, and this cannot be explained in terms of the orthodox view. Individuals cannot be said to exist if the properties (or predicates) they instantiate

---

[11] The problem here is not that the existence of any given property requires the existence of infinitely many other properties. There is nothing inherently objectionable about that—indeed, something like this appears to be manifestly *true* for the existence of numbers. The point I am making is rather about the analysis or explanation of what it is to exist: the viciousness comes in when we try to *analyse* or *explain* what it is for X to exist and find that we must presuppose that we *already* know what it is for Y to exist (where X and Y are both properties here). In general, regresses are only vicious in the context of some explanatory aim, not in themselves.

cannot be said to exist, since the former requires the latter: for x to exist is for there to *exist* some property (or predicate) F such that x instantiates F.

The third objection arises from a family of sentences that resist the orthodox paraphrase. Some of these have become familiar, though their polemical power has been underestimated. In view of the existence of these sentences, there has been a tendency to declare that 'exists' has two sorts of interpretation, predicative and higher-order. But this bifurcating view is unworkable and we are compelled to take all occurrences of 'exists' as predicative. Thus it has often been pointed out that singular attributions of existence are hard to slot into the orthodox schema, on pain of distorting the semantics of singular terms like demonstratives and proper names: we get pushed towards a description theory of reference for these terms that has internal problems.[12] The point I want to make is that accepting this problem about singular statements cannot but affect the way we view 'exists' in general statements. Consider 'Venus exists and is a planet' and 'at least one planet exists': the former entails the latter. But how can that be if 'exists' in the singular sentence is predicative while in the general sentence it is not? We simply have no term common to premises and conclusion if we bifurcate 'exists' in the suggested way; we must either take the singular sentence to be analysable in the orthodox style or we must revise our views of the general sentence. As I will explain below, I favour treating 'Fs exist' along the lines of 'for some x, x exists and x is F', which allows me to find the common term with the predicative 'exists' in 'a exists'. But my point now is that the orthodox view has to do something to save the entailment—it can't just declare that 'exists' is sometimes predicative and sometimes not. And of course it is deeply unattractive to suppose that 'exists' has the kind of ambiguity the bifurcating account proposes.

[12] See Kripke, *Naming and Necessity*. Kripke discussed the topic of existence and names extensively in his 1973 John Locke Lectures in Oxford, which I attended, but which have not yet been published.

The problems of analysis for the orthodox view are made vivid by the sentence 'something exists'. This is a perfectly meaningful and true sentence, which follows from such sentences as 'Venus exists', but it should itself not exist according to the orthodox view. For it is not paraphrasable within the terms of that view, there being no predicate around to pin the instances on: what property are we saying is instantiated here? The problem is worse than with proper names and demonstratives because at least in their case we could try to appeal to a description theory of singular reference; but there isn't even any reference going on with the word 'something'. If we try to translate the sentence in the standard way we get the gibberish, '$\exists x(\ x)$', with no predicate to write down. You might think we could do better with '$\exists x(\text{Thing}x)$', but this is pleonastic, given the usual meaning of '$\exists x$'. Also, it is unclear what the predicate 'thing' is supposed to mean here if not 'exists'.[13] The natural translation is I think the right one: '$\exists x(\text{Exists}x)$'—'for some

---

[13] A tempting alternative suggestion is that 'something exists' means the same as 'something is self-identical' or 'the property of self-identity has at least one instance'. Thus the formula that captures our recalcitrant sentence is '$(\exists x)(x = x)$', where '$=$' plays the role of the missing predicate. But is this really what 'something exists' *says*? Where is the sign of identity in the original sentence? There is no name to extract it from, as with classic description theories, and it is hard to see how it could plausibly be taken to be expressed by 'something'. Moreover, 'something exists' follows from 'Venus exists', so presumably it will have to be held that the latter sentence means '$(\exists x)(x = \text{Venus})$', thus construing singular existence statements as asserting the identity of something with a named entity. The problem here, in addition to the previous objection, is that such a paraphrase looks irremediably circular, since it presupposes that we already understand what it is for Venus (say) to exist. The invoked predicate '$= \text{Venus}$' embeds the name 'Venus', and the condition will only work to secure existence if this term is taken to refer to an existent entity. Consider '$= \text{Vulcan}$': satisfying this predicate will not secure existence (Vulcan clearly satisfies it!), and the reason is simply that Vulcan does not exist. Satisfying '$= \text{Venus}$' secures existence only because of the existence of Venus, which we were meant to be analysing. I think Russell was aware of this point, which is why he never chose the likes of '$= \text{Venus}$' as the propositional function on which to pin existence. In the case of other predicates, such as 'planet next to Mars', the existence of the property does not depend upon the existence of Venus itself, and hence is not straightforwardly circular in the way '$= \text{Venus}$' is. And there is also the point that bringing in identity in this way undermines a central motivation for the Russellian view, since self-identity has precisely the kind of universality Russell found objectionable in a predicate of existence.

x, *x* exists' (see below for more on this view of '∃*x*'). In any case, it is difficult to see how 'something exists' could succeed in being meaningful on the orthodox view, because it lacks the kind of reference to a property that is required for that view to get a foothold (the same goes for 'nothing exists'). I would regard such unspecific existential sentences as test cases for any theory of existence (they also block metalinguistic analyses along the lines of '"Venus" denotes', since 'something' is not a denoting term). Again, the orthodox view does not have the generality we should expect of a theory of existence.

The fourth objection focuses on the requirement that any existent thing should fall under some property or other. This implies that nothing *could* exist that failed to fall under some property—other than existence, obviously. To exist is to be an instance of a property, so necessarily whatever exists has at least one property. This rules out, as a matter of the meaning of 'exists', the possibility of what we might call 'bare existence'—a thing that exists *without* having any (further) properties. What should we think of this alleged possibility? The question seems to be a substantive metaphysical question, open to rational debate. Maybe bare existence is actually a metaphysical impossibility, though how one might argue for that is not clear.[14] But, in any case, it does not appear to be analytic or tautological to assert that bare existence is impossible—which it would have to be according to the orthodox view. It would have to be equivalent to saying, 'there could not be an instance of a property that was not an instance of a property'. That is, it would have to be *contradictory* to assert the possibility of bare existence, as in 'an instance of a property could be an instance of no property'. This is simply because existence is being analysed

---

[14] Again, we have the question of what to say about self-identity: is it contradictory to suppose that an object exists and lacks even the property of self-identity? This does seem to me quite impossible, but I am not convinced that it is actually formally contradictory. In any case, it is of no real help to the defender of the Russellian thesis, since this seems precisely the wrong kind of property to invoke in order to analyse what it means to say that something exists, for the reasons mentioned in the previous footnote.

as property instantiation, so we could not then go on to say that the existent thing has *no* properties. But it seems to me that there is no actual contradiction in the idea of bare existence, even though it may well be some sort of metaphysical impossibility: '*x* exists and *x* has no properties' certainly does not *appear* to be a straightforwardly self-refuting sentence. I think the idea of an object that has *only* the property of existence is not intrinsically self-defeating, but it would have to be if existence simply consisted in property instantiation.

Actually, the problem here spreads, because the orthodox view requires, not merely that every existent object have some property, but also that it have some property *unique* to it. For the existence of an individual object is said to consist in the instantiation of a property sufficient for *that object* to exist and not some other object. Thus the theory characteristically claims that some definite description or individual concept is instantiated, this serving to single out the individual in question. But this implies that in every possible world in which an individual exists that individual has some property that no other individual has. Surely that is a very strong claim, and not one that we ought to be obliged to accept just by the simple analysis of the concept of existence.[15] The analysis of existence ought to be neutral on the point. On the face of it, there seems no logical bar to a range of individuals existing in a world without there being a property that singles each of them out uniquely—as it might be, a collection of indiscernible red steel spheres. We surely don't want our theory of existence to settle the vexed question of

---

[15] Of course, identity with an object is always a property unique to it, as with '=Venus'; but as we have seen, this is not the right kind of property to use in characterizing existence: the individuating property must be one that does not itself presuppose the existence of the entity in question. There is also the point that if we insist on using self-identity as the property that is uniquely instantiated in the case of assertions of singular existence, then we disconnect such assertions from assertions of general existence, as with 'tigers exist'. We don't want to end up saying that the existence of each individual tiger consists in its instantiating identity with itself but that the existence of tigers in general consists in instantiating the property of being a tiger. The restriction to the self-identity property looks ad hoc, designed simply to secure uniqueness.

the necessary identity of indiscernibles. And why should existence necessarily attach to the property, if there is one, which the object happens uniquely to instantiate, instead of all the other properties the object has? It certainly does not seem contradictory to insist that an object could exist that differed in no respect from a numerically distinct object. Yet it would have to be contradictory according to the orthodox view of singular existence statements.

Taken together, these four objections imply that the orthodox view simply has not got hold of the concept of existence. It only seems to have done so for certain limited cases because it pre-supposes the notion of existence, as when it employs the locution 'has instances'. But the theory cannot deal with property existence, it cannot handle the full range of existential statements, and it links the possibility of existence too intimately to the idea of (uniquely) instantiating a property. In short, the concept of existence is not identical to the concept of property instantiation (even though this concept itself invokes the concept of existence). Let me now work out the first-order property view more thoroughly, responding to some questions that might be raised about it.

The property view says that every occurrence of the word 'exists' is logically predicative, just as 'man' and 'blue' are. It also says all existential statements can be analysed by means of this predicate. And this is just the semantic counterpart to the ontological thesis that existence is always and everywhere a property of objects. It is a property universal to all objects that exist, somewhat like self-identity; but it is less universal than identity because (as I noted in the previous chapter) that relation holds of all conceivable objects, not merely those that happen to exist.

What problems might be raised by this simple view? Why has it been so consistently rejected? It is surprisingly difficult to find any worked-out objections to it, despite the suspicions it arouses. The only point that Russell makes, and it is a recurrent theme, is that existence is, so to speak, too universal to be a property: 'There is no sort of point in a predicate which could not conceivably be false. I mean, it is perfectly clear that, if there were such a thing as this existence of individuals that we talk of, it would be absolutely impossible for it not to apply, and that is the characteristic of a mistake.'[16] There are two problems with this argument. First, it proves too much, since self-identity and logical properties (such as the property of not being both red and not red at the same time) are counter-examples to it: these apply to all conceivable objects, but we should hardly wish to analyse them as higher-order properties. And why should there not be such absolutely universal predicates? Can't there be features that all objects share (such as being an object)?[17] There may not be much point in speaking of such properties, given that they have no complement class, but that is not to say that they are not true of everything: there are many truths that are not worth mentioning in ordinary contexts. Second, it is just wrong of Russell to say that 'exists' applies to all conceivable objects and hence has no utility. It precisely does *not* apply to all conceivable objects, since some of the objects we conceive do not exist. Of course, it applies to all objects that *exist*, but we have a good use for the word simply because we make mistakes about existence. The word 'exists' indeed applies to all existent objects and to nothing else, but sometimes we take it to apply when it doesn't.[18] It can be extremely useful to be told that something exists

[16] 'The Philosophy of Logical Atomism', 241.

[17] Or 'having properties', or 'standing in relation to something', or 'being nameable'. In fact, Russell himself has to invoke such a universal property to make his theory work, namely 'being an instance of some property or other': since existence consists in instantiating some property, he has to presuppose that every existent object has some property or other to which its existence attaches. Indeed, it is hard to see how such universality could be avoided if we are to find an analysis of existence that applies to every case.

[18] This is why it is a mistake to think that true singular statements of existence must be trivial and false ones contradictory, on the grounds that reference itself presupposes existence. The reason this is a mistake is simply that the audience for existential assertions may not *know* that a given singular term refers to something that exists, so that it is informative to couple such a term with a predication of existence. If we are discussing planets and I say, 'Venus exists but Vulcan does not', this can be informative to

when you had supposed that it does not (and vice versa). So this objection from generality fails to cut much ice.

There are two main areas in which the predicate view needs careful handling and where it might be thought to run into trouble: the interpretation of the quantifiers and the nature of non-existence. I shall deal with these in turn.

We have become accustomed to speaking of the 'existential quantifier' and to supposing that it conveys existence in a non-predicative fashion; thus we suppose that existence is not always expressed as a predicate. As I pointed out, this divided position is unstable, especially in view of the entailments that need to be captured. But, more fundamentally, the view is misconceived at root: for it may be that '∃x' is rightly defined by using the existence predicate, so that it is not an *alternative* to the predicate view. And I think it is easy to show that it *can* be defined in this way; also that this is intuitively the right way to think about it. Take the formula 'for some x, x is F and x exists', and take this to translate '*F*s exist'. The point here is that the prefix 'for some x' does not itself carry existential import; it simply conveys how many things are being said to be thus and so. Now I claim that this formula conveys the sense of the existential statement, and it expresses existence predicatively. What the prefix does is indicate the *quantity* of *F*s in question—it says that some are; it is left up to the predicate 'exists' to express existence. The word 'some' by itself is existentially neutral, on this view, much as 'all' is usually taken to be[19]—and I

you precisely because you do not know which of 'Venus' and 'Vulcan' is the empty term. Of course, *I* know, because I am aware of the existential facts, and so the statement is not informative to *me*—but no statement is informative to me in *that* sense, because I already know the fact I am stating. My audience may be clueless about matters of existence, so they are unapprised of the semantic status of the singular terms I use; what they learn from my existential assertions is that those terms either refer to something that exists or not, as the case may be. See David Pears, 'Is Existence a Predicate?' for a formulation of the kind of argument I am here rejecting.

[19] I mean here that it is customary to take 'all men are mortal' as existentially neutral on account of the material conditional embedded in it. It is true that in standard logic '$(\forall x)(Fx)$' implies '$(\exists x)(Fx)$', but it is deemed correct to regard typical universal state-

would say the same for 'most', 'many', 'a few', as they occur in statements of existence, as in 'most superheroes exist'. To defend this
view I need to suggest a plausible semantics for the conjunctive
formula and to motivate this way of thinking about quantifier words.

I can think of three possible sorts of interpretation for the formula, which are not unfamiliar. First, we could introduce a
Meinongian ontology, letting the variables range over subsistent as
well as existent entities. Then the conjunction says of these entities that some both exist (as opposed to subsist) and are *F*. On this
interpretation, 'for some x' has ontological import but not existential import, since not everything in our Meinongian ontology
exists; 'exists' then narrows down the ontological field among all
the *F*s there are. Second, we could go substitutionalist and deprive
'for some x' of any objectual function: the formula then says only
that 'x' can be replaced with a term 't' such that 't exists and t is F'
comes out true. That is, we interpret 'some' purely substitutionally
in the standard way, then we introduce existence by means of an
explicit predicate. On this interpretation, '$\exists x$' simply abbreviates
the substitutional quantifier plus its appended existence predicate;
we thus break apart the existential and the quantitative aspects of
the complex symbol '$\exists x$'. Third, we could introduce a special
quantifier expression that is equivalent to 'some of the things we
talk/think about' (what we might call the 'intentional quantifier')
and then append existence in the usual way. Thus '*F*s exist' means:
'some of the things we talk/think about are both *F* and exist'; sym-
bolically, 'Ix, x is F and x exists', where 'Ix' is the intentional quantifier.[20] The function of 'some', again, is purely to convey the

---

ments as lacking existential import in virtue of the possible vacuous truth of the
embedded conditional. What I am suggesting, then, is that a similar leniency should
be applied to our use of 'some'. I will happily accept that 'all' implies 'some', as in
standard logic, but I deprive 'some' of existential import: if all the gods are tyrannical,
then indeed some are—but of course no gods exist.

[20] As I have defined it here the intentional quantifier ranges only over objects of
reference. If we want to include objects that exist and have not been referred to, then
we can simply make the quantifier disjunctive and include in its domain both intentional objects and those ordinary objects that exist without ever being referred to. In

quantity of things that we talk about that both exist and are *F*. We could thus quite meaningfully say, 'for some *x* that we talk about, *x* does not exist': this would follow, for example, from the truth that Vulcan does not exist. On this interpretation, to be (to exist) is emphatically not to be the value of a variable. The idea here is to interpret the variable so that its values are both existent entities and merely intentional ones, where a merely intentional object does not even subsist (I shall have much more to say about non-existent intentional objects shortly). So it seems that we can assign a coherent and plausible interpretation to our formula and hence show that the 'existential quantifier' is analysable in terms of the predicate of existence. I think this is intuitively right, and it solves the problem of the univocity of existence statements. We also see that in adopting the predicate view we can preserve our usual logic of quantifiers, suitably interpreted; we don't need to go back to old-fashioned logic in which '*F*s exist' is a subject–predicate statement with '*F*s' figuring as the subject. In 'some men exist' it is not that 'some men' is the subject and 'exists' the predicate, which gives rise to notorious absurdities with 'no men exist'; we can hang on to the standard paraphrase that treats 'some' as a second-order predicate, not as a singular term.[21] Existence is always predicated of individuals, not of mysterious pluralities.

But is this a *good* way to think about 'some'? Does 'some', taken by itself, really lack existential import in ordinary language? This is quite a big question, but I think there are clear considerations in its favour—it is not merely that it is required by the correct theory of existence. To begin with, quantifier words are precisely that—they tell you how many, what proportion. But that is not an inherently

this way the universal intentional quantifier can range over real and fictional objects in 'all men are mortal'—in which case that statement turns out false by dint of immortal fictional characters. We can then rely on conversational context to convey suitable implicatures when we want to speak only of real people.

[21] Notice that 'some' is treated as second-order while 'exists' is treated as first-order; so it is wrong to reason that since 'some' is a second-order concept 'exists' must also be. The question of the semantic level of quantifier words is orthogonal to the issue of whether existence is predicative.

existential concern. We do better to call 'some' the *partial* quantifier, on analogy with the universal quantifier—neither logically
implies existence. The same should be said of the non-standard
quantifiers, 'most', 'many', etc. In the orthodox notion expressed by
'$\exists x$' we have conflated two distinct linguistic functions into the '$\exists x$'
symbol—the function of saying how many and the function of
implying existence (and the name 'existential quantifier' only captures this latter aspect). But, as we have separated these functions
for 'all', so we should for 'some'.[22] And this fits the linguistic data,
because we do use 'some' in contexts in which existence is not
implied, even conversationally. Thus we can say, 'some of the
things you're talking about don't exist', 'some superheroes are
entirely fictional', 'some cities are purely imaginary'. In these sentences 'some' expresses a proportion, but it does not imply that this
proportion exists—quite the opposite, since the predicates negate
existence. If you try to translate these uses of 'some' into the existential quantifier, so called, you get outright contradictions. Better
to take 'some' neutrally and then leave it to 'exists' to do what it
does best—assert existence.

On this view, 'some' only acquires existential force as a matter of
conversational implicature. But this implicature can be cancelled
without contradiction, as when one annoyingly says 'some of the
things I've just been referring to don't exist' or (less annoyingly)
'some of the gods are tempestuous, but of course no gods exist'. A
similar point can be made about the word 'object': it can seem that
this word carries an implication of existence, so that speaking of
non-existent objects sounds contradictory, especially when you lay
stress on the word 'object'. But I think it is clear that this is a mere
implicature, since we do use the word quite correctly to speak of

---

[22] So I am going further than free logic in stripping quantificational logic of existential assumptions. Where free logic gives up existential generalization, I give up the
existential import of the sign for partial quantification itself, i.e. 'some'. We therefore
can infer 'someone is a detective' from 'Sherlock Holmes is a detective', even though
Sherlock Holmes does not exist. As a matter of strict logic, then, it is never possible to
infer existence from anything (except existence itself, of course), not even a sentence
of partial quantification.

'objects of thought'. When we use the word in this kind of context all suggestions of existence are cancelled. If I speak of the object of your search as the fountain of youth, there is no implication of existence here. It is the same with 'some': most of the time the implicature is in force, since generally we mean to be speaking of existent things, and this is common knowledge between us; but the general implicature can in principle be cancelled, and then 'some' shows its true semantic colours as a device of pure quantification, with no existential entailments.[23] This is why we can quite happily say, 'some objects (of thought) do not exist'. On this view, it is not that when 'some' occurs without existential force it is always somehow embedded in an intentional context which erases its customary existential punch; rather, it packs no such punch as a matter of its semantics (as opposed to its pragmatics) but serves purely to express quantity or proportion—just like 'all'. If you want to get existence semantically into the picture you have to say so. This is why it is not pleonastic to say 'some tame tigers exist', and not contradictory to say 'some superheroes do not exist'. In other words, the linguistic appearances are a true guide to semantic reality: 'some' does not in fact contain 'exists', implicitly or explicitly, which is just how it appears. Accordingly, we need 'exists' in the language in addition to 'some'—which is exactly what we find. What quantifier words do is abandon singularity; what 'exists' does is attribute the property of existence to objects that are either denoted or quantified over. It invites confusion to try to merge these two functions together into a single primitive symbol '$\exists x$'. The phrase 'existential quantifier' obscures this point: think how odd it sounds to call 'all' the existential quantifier just because you

[23] Imagine teaching a literature class in which various fictional characters are being discussed (I do this quite often). You say, 'some of the characters in *Lolita* are despicable', and go on to discuss their personal failings. This is perfectly good English and clearly the context excludes existential implications. Now imagine switching to a context of real criminal investigation; here it will be assumed that you are talking of real people when you say, 'some of these car thieves are pretty smart'. But surely the word 'some' does not shift its literal meaning from one context to the next; it is simply a matter of the implicatures carried by the context of utterance.

believe, as some have, that it too implies existence. To label 'some' the existential quantifier is not simply to describe its function but to impose a tendentious theory upon it, a theory that we have seen to be false to the linguistic data. Matters would be much clearer if we spoke of the universal quantifier and the partial quantifier. We can, of course, just define an expression '∃x' that contains both notions, as we have in effect traditionally done; but we should be aware of what the correct semantic analysis of such a stipulated expression consists in—and we should be wary of taking this symbol to translate the natural language 'some'.

The topic of non-existence engages more purely metaphysical concerns, and it is true that the topic can quickly generate bewilderment and confusion; truisms turn into absurdities in the blink of an eye. The problem, put crudely, is to make sure that things that don't exist don't end up existing after all. The predicate 'exists' fails to apply to some things—what we have to ensure is that these things don't turn out to exist in some attenuated or second-class way: they simply *don't exist*. I think it is essential, in avoiding this danger, to acknowledge a crucial asymmetry between existence and non-existence, namely that non-existence is representation-dependent, while existence is not. That is, the complement class of 'exists' is purely intentional—its *esse* is *concipi*. The Meinongian ontology of non-existence implicitly denies this, holding that merely subsistent entities could have Being even though they have never been conceived. But I want to say that there are no mind-independent non-existent entities—though there are plenty of mind-independent existent entities. Compare a predicate like 'blue': there can be blue things we have not encountered cognitively, but there can also be non-blue things we have not encountered—and similarly for every other ordinary predicate. If we think of the complement class of 'exists' in this way, then we will hold that there could be objects that don't exist and have not been thought of, since their nature does not consist in their being conceived. But this strikes me as a fundamental misconception: there are no non-existent things that transcend our cognitive acts;

all non-existent things are objects of thoughts, as a matter of necessity.[24] And this marks a deep contrast with typical predicates. Not that this shows that 'exists' is not a predicate after all, but it does tell us something important about how the concept works. When we say that an object does not exist we are ascribing non-existence to a purely intentional object; indeed this is precisely what its non-existence consists in. If it were any other type of object, then it would have existence after all.

This raises the question of the relation between existence and possibility—in particular, whether merely possible objects exist. It seems wrong to insist that all possible objects must be conceived, because this makes possibility into a mind-dependent matter; yet in some sense merely possible objects are ontologically lacking. So are possible objects non-existent and yet mind-independent? And are not fictional objects at least possible objects? Here I side with Saul Kripke's view of non-existent entities like unicorns and Sherlock Holmes: these are not genuinely metaphysically possible objects.[25] The central problem with the possibility interpretation of talk about unicorns and Sherlock Holmes is that there are too many such possible objects, all the ones that answer to the descriptions given in the stories—and which of these is really Holmes or

---

[24] The fundamental reason for this is that non-existent objects are individuated only by the ideas we associate with them. If we are told that a particular something doesn't exist, we need to know *which* thing is being said not to exist—we need a suitable individual concept. The notion of an entity not existing that has no individual concept associated with it is ill-defined: *what* is it, precisely, that does not exist? Fictional characters are the paradigm here: Sherlock Holmes only comes *not* to exist because he is a character created by Arthur Conan Doyle—it is not that there was a well-defined fact of Holmes's non-existence before Conan Doyle ever created the character. As it were, thought and language are what bring non-existent objects into being. Even in the case of general statements of non-existence, such as 'tigers with ten legs do not exist', we cannot say which *particular* such tigers suffer from non-existence without invoking some conceptual individuation. In the case of unconceived existent objects the object itself operates to individuate it, but in the case of alleged unconceived non-existent particular objects there is simply nothing to give them individuation conditions—there is nothing *specific* that fails to exist in such a putative case. This is why particularized non-existent objects are always intentional objects.

[25] *Naming and Necessity*, 156–8.

the unicorns? But this only tells us that fictional entities are not metaphysically possible entities; it does not tell us whether there are *other* possible entities that are non-existent and also mind-independent, contrary to the principle I laid down earlier. To this I reply that merely possible entities, such as the younger sister I might have had, really do exist, and did exist before I ever formed the concept of them—though they do not *actually* exist. Such entities exist in the realm of the merely possible; their ontological deficiency consists just in the fact that their existence is not actual. When we think that they fail to exist we are confusing existence with actual existence, and it is their want of the latter that explains their difference from ordinary objects like the people around me. But I think that fictional entities, like Sherlock Holmes, are not correctly viewed as possible objects analogous to the possible people that would have actually existed had the reproductive facts been different. Of course, such non-existent objects are *epistemically* possible, but they are not metaphysically so. So non-existence is an essential property of Holmes and unicorns, while it is not an essential property of my possible sister. On the other hand, existence is not an essential property of Venus and Clinton. This asymmetry shows that existence, though a genuine property, is different from properties in general: generally, if *F*ness is a contingent property of objects, then so is non-*F*ness—but not so in the case of existence. In sum, then, genuinely possible objects do exist, though not actually, while genuinely non-existent objects have that status necessarily.[26]

---

[26] I am not intending here to persuade the reader that it is correct to view possible objects as existing; I am simply stating what I take to be a familiar view. My purpose is to indicate how the representation-dependence of non-existence can be made consistent with the mind-independence of possibilia—namely, by recognizing that possibilia exist. There may be an element of stipulation in this way of talking, but it serves to protect what otherwise seems a compelling thesis, namely the identification of non-existent with merely intentional objects. Note that none of this is directly relevant to the question of whether existence is a property; the representation-dependence of non-existence is a logically separate thesis.

It might help if I restate my position by considering three different theories of the truth conditions for 'Vulcan does not exist'. First, it might be held that 'Vulcan' stands for a possible object and that possible objects don't exist. Second, it might be held that 'Vulcan' stands for a possible object and that possible objects do exist, and what the statement is really saying is that this existent object does not *actually* exist—thus 'the existent possible object Vulcan is not actual'. Third, it might be held that 'Vulcan' stands for no possible object at all and that the predicative part of the sentence simply ascribes non-existence to this non-existent object. My proposal, then, is to go with this third view, thus cleaving to the thesis that all non-existence is representation-dependent. Possible objects are not counter-examples to this thesis since they involve existence.

But is *impossibility* a counter-example to the thesis? It might be thought both that impossible objects don't exist and that they are not representation-dependent. Round squares don't exist, it may be said, but they are not necessarily objects of thought. Didn't round squares fail to exist in the universe before thinkers ever came along to conceive of them? Aren't there many impossible objects that we have never thought about? This is a puzzling and subtle issue, but I am inclined to take the following line: impossible objects, like possible objects, *do* exist, but what they lack is the possibility of actuality—they are existent entities that *could* not be actual. They have the property of existence but they have it in such a way that they could never have this property actually. Their essence is to exist in modal limbo, necessarily closed off from actualization. This explains our sense that they are fundamentally lacking ontologically, but it is not because they have no existence—it is because their existence is necessarily non-actual. Nor could anything *like* them actually exist, whereas in the case of Holmes and the unicorns, though they lack existence entirely, at least things like them could exist. Distance from actuality, as measured by modal status or dissimilarity to actual things, is not the same as non-existence. Impossible objects are not, then, counter-examples to the thesis that non-existence is always representation-dependent.[27]

It may now be asked how we can ascribe *any* properties to purely intentional objects, including the property of non-existence. Here we need to heed carefully the way we actually talk and not impose misleading models on our concepts. For we simply *do* ascribe properties to non-existent objects—we make remarks about them. Thus we say that Pegasus is a horse not a pig, that Zeus is the senior god, that Sherlock Holmes is a brilliant detective. These statements are all true and they contain predicative expressions; so, yes, we can predicate properties of non-existent entities. Not all predication involves referring to an existent entity and ascribing a property to it; sometimes we take a non-existent entity and ascribe a property to it.[28] This, as Wittgenstein would say, is what we do. Our theories

[27] Again, I do not expect to persuade the reader of this conception of impossible objects, and the issue is certainly highly debatable. By way of nudging intuitions, think of a conversation about whether there are impossible objects as well as possible ones: no one in the conversation has ever thought of such things as round squares, and then someone says, 'yes, there are impossible objects—think of objects that are both round and square!'; there follows general agreement among the discussants that indeed there are such things, after all. Haven't they just agreed that impossible objects *do* exist, though it was hard to think of any examples for a while? These objects are certainly not merely fictional, since the impossibility of round squares obtained independently of anyone conceiving of them or telling a story about them.

This raises the question of whether Sherlock Holmes might be such an existent impossible object. I have said that Holmes is an impossible object, now I say such objects exist, so might not Holmes be one such? My answer is that impossible objects come in two varieties: the existent and the non-existent. We already know that Holmes does not exist, and his impossibility does not disturb this knowledge; but in the case of round squares the matter is up for discussion, and there seem to be grounds for allowing existence to these entities. We at least know what it would *be* for round squares to exist—they are well-defined entities. But in the case of fictional entities we have the problem, noted by Kripke, that there are too many candidates for being Holmes in the space of possible (and impossible!) worlds—his individuation is too underdetermined by the content of the stories. So: some impossibilia exist and some do not. (Of course, I am aware that these are very delicate issues, and that it is not altogether clear *what* to say about them; I am presenting what seems to be the best overall conception of the ontology of these matters.)

[28] Compare ascribing properties to merely possible objects: my possible sister Edith (the one that would have resulted from the combination of a particular sperm and egg) has the property of being female. So it is not only actual objects that have properties.

need to respect this fact not deny it. And if so, there is no bar to ascribing the property of non-existence to some of the things we talk about. Just as Zeus fails to be mortal, so he fails to exist; just as Vulcan fails to be a cactus, so it fails to exist; just as unicorns fail to be two-horned, so they fail to be exist. Imagine someone overhearing a conversation you are having about Vulcan and wondering what you are talking about. 'What is this Vulcan thing anyway?' they ask, and you reply, 'Oh, Vulcan is a planet that some astronomers mistakenly thought to exist.' 'So it's not a cactus you're referring to with the name "Vulcan"?' 'Definitely not, Vulcan is a planet not a cactus—and moreover it doesn't exist.' Here we see properties asserted and denied of a non-existent entity, among them existence itself. As a general rule, intentional objects have just those properties our mental acts confer on them; this is why it sounds so odd to suggest that Pegasus is really a fluffy poodle not a winged horse.

But there is another approach to assertions of non-existence, which might be prompted by disquietude at the idea that non-existent objects can be genuine subjects of predication, at least in a primitive way. We want to ask what it *is* for an object to fail to exist; we want some analysis of this. To exist is to have the simple property of existence, but non-existence seems to be a matter of our failed intentionality, if I may put it thus. Given that non-existence is representation-dependent, we should be able to explain it in those terms. Thus we might suppose that there is some complexity in such statements, and that they make reference to cognitive acts in some way. There are two main cases to consider: fiction and empirical postulation. The idea, then, is that when I say, 'Holmes does not exist' I am saying something like this: 'it is just a fictional pretence that Holmes exists'; and when I say, 'Vulcan does not exist' I am saying something like this: 'it was a mistaken postulation

---

In the case of fictional objects the origin and foundation of their properties is the story that refers to them; hence we can say quite correctly that Holmes is a detective, thereby predicating a property of Holmes. And clearly the predicate 'detective' is not ambiguous in factual and fictional contexts.

that Vulcan exists'. In these paraphases 'exists' occurs only in its positive form, and the denial of existence is carried by the implication that cognitive acts of make-believe or mistaken postulation have occurred. Putting both together, the basic truth condition of the negative existential is that there was only an entertaining of existence. And we cannot further explain this by saying that the object of the entertaining does not exist; the end of line comes with the statement that this was a case of mere entertaining. Non-existence is essentially and constitutively failed intentionality, whereas existence is not definable as successful intentionality. Existence is having a mind-independent property, but non-existence results from the occurrence of a certain kind of mental act—a pretence or an erroneous postulation of existence. Assertions of non-existence really are statements about mental acts, just as the representation-dependence thesis suggests.[29] This makes non-existence very different from non-squareness, say: to assert

[29] When I say this I do not mean to be asserting that statements of non-existence *mean* the same as statements about failed intentionality; I am speaking rather of the basic truth-maker for negative existentials. Analogies are always potentially misleading, but we can compare this to the secondary quality conception of colour: what makes it true that an object is red is that it is disposed to look red to perceivers, but it is not that 'red' *means* (is synonymous with) 'disposed to look red'; rather, the disposition is what redness ontologically consists in—or redness supervenes on such a disposition (see my 'Another Look at Colour' on this). Similarly, the non-existence of Holmes depends upon the occurrence of certain creative mental acts that have no target in the real world; if you like, such non-existence is supervenient on mental acts that have no real world reference. This view is quite compatible with acknowledging that the concept of failed intentionality must be analysed by invoking the concept of non-existence—failed intentionality is precisely a case in which the intentional object *does not exist*. In the case of colour 'looks red' contains the word 'red', but that does not show that redness is not supervenient on dispositions to look red. My claim about non-existence is not that failed intentionality is conceptually prior to non-existence; it is the claim that facts of non-existence obtain in virtue of failed intentionality, in the sense that there is no non-existence without failed intentionality. This marks the difference between existence and non-existence, since existence is not supervenient on successful intentionality. Existence is like a primary quality; non-existence is like a secondary quality. So we don't have to regard the non-existence of an object as a bedrock fact with no further articulation; we can say what is involved in an object's (so to speak) coming not to exist.

Alternatively, we could stick with the simple idea that non-existence is just primitively one of the properties that Sherlock Holmes has in addition to being a detective.

that an object is not square is not to assert that it was mistakenly taken to be square, since that may not be so and anyway is not what the statement means. There is no allusion here to erroneous mental acts. But to say that an object does not exist *is* to allude to mistaken suppositions or acts of make-believe. I think this asymmetry is entirely intuitive: non-existence really does have a lot more to do with misfirings of the mind than do other kinds of property lack. I suspect that it is the nature of non-existence—its difference from other kinds of property lack—that is at the root of the old feeling that existence cannot be a property like any other. The negation of existence works differently from the negation of other properties, because of the underlying representation-dependence of non-existence; but we should not infer from this that existence itself is not a simple first-order property of objects. Thus we can explain the feeling that existence is a peculiar sort of property while not withdrawing the claim that this is nevertheless what it is. To be a peculiar or even unique kind of property is not to fail to be a property.

There is a further reason someone might have for doubting the predicate view, which is epistemological in character: namely, that existence is not a *perceptible* property of objects. If we hold to the empiricist principle that the only properties of objects are perceptible properties, at least in principle, then we get the result that existence isn't a property, at least on some plausible assumptions. (Russell, of course, was strongly empiricist in his general outlook, so he may well have been influenced by this consideration: where in my sense-datum of a table, he might have asked, is the quality of existence?) Why is existence not a perceptible feature of objects? Because regardless of whether or not an object exists it will still present the same sensory appearance: hallucinated pink rats look an awful lot like existent pink rats. A non-existent object can appear just as an existent object does. Being blue, say, makes a difference to how something looks, so that blue rats look quite unlike pink ones: but existing makes no qualitative difference—there is no *impression* of existence (as Hume in effect said). This is really why scepticism about the external world is possible: you can never build existence into the appearances, so it must always be inferred or assumed. If existence were like colour, you could know that the external world exists just by inspecting your sense-data: but that is exactly what existence does not allow. I know that my current intentional object is blue and circular, but I have nothing sensory to guarantee that it also exists.

The right response to this point about imperceptibility is to concede the premiss but deny that the conclusion follows: true, existence is not a perceptible property, but it does not follow that it is not a property—it is just a rather special property. Is self-identity a perceptible property of objects, or logical and modal properties? Apparently not, but then why should existence be? Empiricism of this kind is just mistaken, a misguided assimilation of everything real to the perceptible. To deny that existence is a property on account of its imperceptibility is just a hyperbolic reaction to its specific character. It is a property that is universal to what exists, whose complement class is representation-dependent, and which is not perceptible: that is its nature. So there is no cogent objection here to the view that existence functions as a first-order property of objects.

I now want to consider three specific contexts in which the concept of existence is essentially invoked; my purpose is to show the superiority of the predicate view over the orthodox view in handling these contexts.

(i) The *Cogito*. Consider the statement 'I exist': how should we analyse it? On the face of it, this is a subject–predicate statement consisting of an indexical singular term and a term that ascribes a property to the referent of that indexical (in a context). And I maintain that this is precisely what it is, logically speaking. This is the default position, barring arguments to the contrary. But how does the orthodox view handle it? It needs to find a predicate for 'exists' to attach to; but no such predicate apparently figures there;

so one has to be contrived. Thus we are pushed towards a description theory of 'I', which will enable us to say that the proposition that I exist is equivalent to the proposition that a description *D* has a unique instance. But there are well-known problems with this, since any natural description will fail to have the force of the indexical.[30] I can know, for example, that the description 'the author of *The Mysterious Flame*' has a unique satisfier without realizing that I am that author, so indexical and description do not mean the same.[31] The only remotely workable description will be metalinguistic, like 'the referent of *this* (token of) "I"', so that the *Cogito* is saying in effect that '*x* is a referent of this (token of) "I"' is uniquely instantiated. Now that does not look much like what the original statement says: the *Cogito* is less convoluted than that; it is not metalinguistic; it could be stated by someone incapable of semantic ascent; it has a transparent certainty the paraphrase lacks. But there is also a clear logical problem, because we are now referring to *two* things—the self and a token of 'I'—and both have to exist for the statement to be true. So we are presupposing the truth of 'this token of "I" exists', which contains an indexical referring to a word token—and how is *that* to be analysed? We will need another definite description: but that will either contain an indexical or it won't. If it does, then we need another description to explain the existence of *its* referent; if it does not, then we fail to produce something with the semantic force of the original, since indexicality cannot be captured non-indexically. The same point applies if we replace 'I' with 'the bearer of *these* mental states',

---

[30] What about invoking self-identity again in the shape of the predicate '= I'? Then we could say that 'I exist' means '$(\exists x)(x = I)$', which latter inherits the semantic properties of the original indexical. But, again, this presupposes my existence, since the term 'I' must be taken to refer to an existent entity—me—in the context '= I'. We do not explain what it is for me to exist by stating that someone is identical to me. Nor, intuitively, is this what I mean when I say that I exist—where is the identity sign to be found in that sentence? And there is also the point I made at the beginning, that the idea of an *instance* of '= I' already builds in the notion of existence, since Sherlock Holmes cannot be allowed to count as an instance of self-identity if this is to be sufficient for existence.   [31] See John Perry, 'The Problem of the Essential Indexical'.

referring to my own mental states: this presupposes the truth of 'these mental states exist', and this cannot be analysed non-indexically. The point here is that the irreducibility of indexicals, especially the 'I' of the *Cogito*, is inconsistent with the orthodox analysis of singular existentials in terms of descriptions. If the only way to preserve the special semantic properties of 'I' is to introduce some new indexical, then we need to explain the corresponding existence statement, which presents the same irresolvable dilemma. So the case is even worse here than for existence statements containing proper names. The lesson is that the *Cogito* cannot be formulated using the orthodox analysis of existence; it needs the predicate treatment.

(ii) Essentialism. A natural way to express essentialist claims employs the notion of existence: for Clinton to be necessarily a man is for it to be the case that Clinton could not exist without being a man. Generally, 'x is essentially F' means 'necessarily, if x exists, x is F'. Now let us ask how the orthodox view would analyse this latter sentence. There are two possibilities: either we use 'F' itself as the predicate to which existence attaches, or we introduce a new predicate. Suppose we use 'F' itself: then we get 'necessarily, if x is an instance of Fness, x is F'. This would be a way of formulating the claim that (say) every man is such that, necessarily, if he exists, he is a man; and it says that every man is such that, necessarily, if he is an instance of manhood, then he is a man. But this, of course, is a plain tautology, which the original statement is not—so they cannot mean the same. We thus need to find some predicate distinct from that which is being declared essential to the objects in question. That will not in general be impossible to do: Clinton, say, satisfies the predicate 'US president in 1999'. This raises Kripkean problems about whether we can preserve modal status under such an analysis, but the point I want to make is different and parallels the point I made earlier about bare existence. It is that the orthodox doctrine now entails that nothing can have an essential property F unless it instantiates *other* properties (not including existence). But is that really a metaphysical necessity?

Couldn't an object have just one property and have it essentially? More to the point, is the denial of this something that an essentialist claim *entails*? Is it *contradictory* to say '*x* is essentially *F* and *x* has no properties other than *F*'? I don't see that it is, but the orthodox analysis implies that it must be, once the tautological translation is ruled out. If we take 'exists' to be a predicate, on the other hand, then we can say simply that for Clinton to have the property of existing he must also have the property of being a man, and this is neither tautologous nor committed to the idea that Clinton must have some *further* property. But if we take existence to attach to a property, in the orthodox way, then we are committed to Clinton having properties other than that of being a man. He does, of course, but my point is that this is not something that the essentialist claim should logically imply, since it is not contradictory to say that an object is essentially *F* and yet has no further properties. I therefore conclude that the orthodox analysis cannot properly handle the use of existence in expressing essentialist claims, while the predicate view has no trouble with this.

(iii) The Ontological Argument. The standard objection to the ontological argument (OA) is that it assumes that existence is a property. Clearly, I am committed to saying that this is a bad objection; so the question for me is what to say about the claim that the definition of God implies his existence. Now I think it was always suspicious to pin the fallacy of the argument on treating existence as a property instead of as a second-order concept, as if we just hadn't noticed that 'exists' is logically on a par with 'numerous'. That is like saying that the argument depends upon a scope confusion or affirming the consequent or some such logical howler. But surely the argument is more interesting and substantive than that diagnosis allows; it is not some simple logical fallacy—pleasant as it might be to think this. Second, it seems to me quite unclear that the argument cannot be reformulated using 'exists' in the second-order way. Thus we can ask whether it is part of God's definition that his attributes must have at least one instance. Does 'being all-powerful and all-knowing and all-good' have to have an instance?

For if it did not, then wouldn't it fail to express the concept of the most perfect being? The concept 'being a perfect being' has to have an instance or else it would not be the concept it purports to be. Third, we should note that the argument can be deployed in the opposite direction to prove the non-existence of the most *imperfect* being. Call that being 'Satan': then Satan cannot exist because he is the most imperfect conceivable being, and existence is one of the perfections. To exist and be imperfect is to be less imperfect than a maximally imperfect being who fails to exist. Thus the most imperfect conceivable being cannot exist. Whatever is wrong with these arguments is independent of whether existence is a property; the logical status of 'exists' is irrelevant.

How can the OA and its Satanic counterpart be resisted? I don't need to answer this in order to defend the property view of existence, but I will make some observations about it anyway. One might think that the weakness lies in the assumption that existence is a perfection and non-existence an imperfection. That is certainly questionable on any natural interpretation of the notion of perfection. But actually we can formulate the argument without using this premiss, by appealing to other aspects of God's definition. He is also the most impressive and most powerful being, by definition. But surely, it will be argued, you cannot be the most impressive and powerful being conceivable if you fail to exist; another being who was just like you but did exist would have to be more impressive and powerful. Thus existence is part of God's definition by virtue of these attributes and not merely by virtue of the notion of perfection. Equally, we can prove that the least impressive and powerful being conceivable could not exist (he will not be the devil, as traditionally conceived), since if a being is defined as the most minimally impressive and powerful being conceivable he could not exist given that existence augments one's impressiveness and power. It is true that this argument sounds strange and sophistical, but it is hard to put one's finger on what exactly is going wrong.

My own suspicion, which is outside the scope of the topic of existence, so I won't try to pursue it here, is that the fault lies in taking notions like 'the most perfect, impressive and powerful being conceivable' to be well-defined. We can make sense of being the most perfect being that exists, and we know what conceivability is, so we think we know what is meant by combining them. But we are lapsing into disguised nonsense here, analogous to the idea of (say) the most perfect conceivable triangle or piece of music or meal. Here too we may know what it is to be the most perfect triangle to exist (construed as an actual drawing), or the best piece of music, or the best meal—and we also know what it means to conceive of one of the things as being superior to another. But it does not follow—and it looks peculiar—to say that there is then a well-defined concept of the most perfect *conceivable* item of any of these types. Suppose I call the most perfect meal conceivable 'Bill': can I infer that Bill exists because if it did not then there would have to be a meal that was conceivably better than Bill? We just don't know what it would *be* to be the most perfect conceivable meal or piece of music. Similarly, the notion of, say, the most powerful conceivable mouse makes little sense; or the most impressive conceivable daisy. This seems to me the place to look for the error in the OA, not in some supposed mistake about the logical character of existence. We can let God have that property so long as his definition really warrants it—but that is what is not at all clear. The problem with the OA, then, is that it trades on notions of the maximal forms of certain attributes, particularly perfection, that are inherently ill-defined.

I conclude that 'exists' is a predicate and that it expresses a property just as other predicates do (whatever properties are and whatever it is for predicates to express them). There is no good objection to this view, and the alternative to it is full of difficulties. It is a word we can correctly apply to individuals, which is just what the surface form of our existential sentences suggests. It has its peculiarities, of course, but they merely tell us what kind of property it is. As so often, the way a word is semantically turns out to be the way it appears to be syntactically (compare proper names).

This is quite compatible with maintaining that 'tigers exist' says that 'tiger' has instances, since the relevant notion of instance is simply that of an object that has the (first-order) property of existence. The orthodox view has inflated a correct point about general statements of existence into the incorrect denial that existence is a property. So we can keep all that is good and wholesome in the logical tradition while not rejecting the obvious. By all means analyse general statements of existence in terms of the 'existential quantifier', but do not make the mistake of inferring that existence is not a predicate just because this analysis works. The existence of tigers consists in the fact that tigers severally have the property of existence; this is what *grounds* the fact that the concept *tiger* has instances and hence makes true '$(\exists x)(x$ is a tiger)'.[32]

---

[32] Thus singular existential facts are basic relative to general existential facts, as we generally suppose for singular and general facts: 'a is F' is what makes true 'something is F'. The Russellian doctrine, by contrast, does not allow this obvious parallelism with singular and general facts in general.

3. PREDICATION

PREDICATES, we are taught, have extensions—the class of objects of which the predicate is true. That seems hard to deny, putting aside special issues like vagueness: if predicates can be true of objects, then there ought to be a set of objects of which the predicate is true. But a stronger claim is commonly made: that these extensions constitute a semantically relevant feature of predicates. A sentence formed from a predicate and a name is said to be true if and only if the object referred to by the name is a member of the set that forms the extension of the predicate (and similarly for other types of sentence structure). Thus it becomes natural to say, as Quine does, that a predicate has 'divided reference' or 'multiplicity of reference': it refers in a plural manner.[1] As a name refers to a single object, so a predicate refers severally to the members of a collection of many objects. Predicates refer to each of the many objects they are true of; so there are as many references for a predicate as there are objects of which it is true. The sense of a predicate may possess a unity or singularity, but its reference is a scattered and multiple affair. Since a predicate is true of many dispersed things, its reference is a distributed totality. On this conception, then, a predicate is not a singular term in Quine's sense: 'a singular term names or purports to name just one object . . . while a general term is true of each, severally, of many objects'.[2] Predicates are classified as *general* terms precisely because they do not refer uniquely to a single entity but generally to a range of entities. It is the multiplicity inherent in predicate reference that is held to mark predicates off from names and other properly singular terms.

[1] See Quine, *Word and Object*, 90 ff.   [2] Ibid. 90–1.

This conception has become so ingrained that we are not apt to notice that it is in fact a substantive theory about the semantics of predicates and their distinction from naming devices. But there is another way of looking at predicates that gives a very different picture of their semantics, namely that predicates refer singularly to properties. The predicate 'red' refers to the property of being red, not to the many red objects the world happens to contain. I venture to suggest that this is the natural way to conceive of predicates, as opposed to the standard extensional view. On this natural view, then, predicates are taken to refer to properties or qualities or attributes—universals in the traditional sense. These properties are not to be identified with extensions: they are not sets of objects but the attributes that form such sets. Thus 'red' refers initially to the property of redness, and those objects that have this property constitute the set of red things. According to this conception, a predicate does not divide its reference at all, since its reference is a property that is just as 'singular' as the object referred to by a regular name. The truth conditions of simple subject–predicate sentences are given accordingly: a sentence of the form 'Fa' is true if and only if the object referred to by the name has the property referred to by the predicate. There is then no reason to withhold the title of singular term from predicates: they name (refer to, designate) just one entity—the property they are used to ascribe to objects. There is no multiplicity or division of reference here—just a unique entity of the universal kind. Predicates do not refer to what they are true of, but to the properties that are instantiated by the things they are true of: the 'true of' relation and the 'refers' relation are distinct relations.

Which of these two views is preferable?[3] It might well seem that the standard view has this advantage—that a predicate at least *has*

---

[3] It might be said that we do not need to choose: predicates refer *both* to the property they express *and* to the members of their extension. But, as I will argue below, we could say the same of names, and hence could equally claim that names have 'divided reference', thus losing their semantic distinctness from predicates. In any case, once we allow properties as referents we hardly need to reckon with extensions. This is why the two conceptions of predicate reference are traditionally taken to be rivals—considerations of semantic redundancy.

an extension distinct from any other reference it might be supposed to have, while a name has no extension over and above the object it refers to. So, putting aside ontological worries about properties for now, the semantics of predicates differs crucially from that of names: even accepting properties as the reference of predicates, there is another semantic level that needs to be acknowledged—the extension of the predicate. With names there is just the named object (and possibly also the sense of the name), but with predicates there is the named property *and* the class of things that have this property. So predicates differ fundamentally from names in virtue of the multiplicity inherent in their extensions. Quine is right *even if* predicates refer to properties, since there are still extensions to reckon with; he has still put his finger on what marks predicates off from names. Suppose we agree that predicates express senses and refer to properties; then there is still their extension left over as an extra layer of semantic reality. But in the case of names, it appears, once we have distinguished their sense and reference we have exhausted their semantic description.[4] Herein lies the basic distinction between the name and the predicate. And if we need extensions anyway why bother to invoke the properties that allegedly mediate between a predicate and what it is true of?

I am going to argue against this position. Ultimately, I wish to defend the natural property view against the standard extension view; but my immediate aim is to undermine the argument just offered. My strategy will be to show that names have the same kind of semantic duality that predicates are taken to have, once the matter is viewed impartially. To establish this I shall present what may well look like a formal trick, using this to argue that the entire

[4] Thus names have a two-level semantic analysis corresponding to sense and reference, while predicates are taken to have a three-level analysis, corresponding to sense, reference, and extension. In Fregean terms, predicates are taken to express a sense, refer to a (first-level) function ('concept'), and have an extension. I shall be arguing that this common distinction between two- and three-level semantic analyses, held to distinguish names from predicates, is arbitrary and unmotivated.

standard framework of extensional semantics is unmotivated and deeply flawed. We have been hoodwinked by a prejudice, not seeing what is really an arbitrary stipulation for what it is. I intend to loosen the hold of some familiar and unexamined assumptions by setting up an alternative semantic framework in which the usual picture is totally inverted.

Take the name 'Bertrand Russell': this name refers to a certain concrete individual, now dead, who is customarily reckoned to be the extension or reference of the name. This object is taken to be the 'semantic value' of the name—the entity invoked in giving the truth conditions of sentences containing the name. Now consider the properties instantiated by that object—everything that holds of Russell. Form the set of these properties, and then assign this set to the name, calling the assigned set the 'second-level extension' of the name. Evidently there is such a set, assuming there are properties at all (we shall return to this), and clearly there is a function that takes each (non-empty) name and yields such a set for that name. If the first-level extension exists (Russell, in this case), then the second-level extension also exists (the totality of properties of Russell). Now consider a sentence formed using this name, say 'Russell was bald', and interpret the predicate by assigning a property to it, viz. baldness. Then we can say that the sentence is true if and only if the following condition holds: the property assigned to the predicate is a member of the set that forms the second-level extension of the name. That is to say: 'Russell was bald' is true if and only if baldness is one of the properties Russell had. It is quite evident that this truth condition is correct and is in some sense equivalent to the standard truth condition formulated in terms of objects and predicate extensions. If Russell belongs to the extension of 'bald', then baldness belongs to the second-level extension of 'Russell'. But the two truth conditions employ quite different ontologies; in particular, the extension of 'bald' is not referred to in the new style of truth condition. Instead of objects and sets of objects we have properties and sets of properties. We have, in effect, inverted the usual rule for constructing truth conditions, now treating the predicate as having a singular reference and the name as having a multiple extension. And the implicit question I am thus posing is: why is this new way not just as good as the old way? Why do it with regular extensions rather than with our newfangled second-level extensions? Why not treat the predicate as making specific reference and the name as having a referential plurality, referring severally to each of the properties that constitute its second-level extension?

An immediate reply from those of Quinean inclinations will be that the new truth condition invokes an ontology of properties, and these are 'creatures of darkness'. I have no sympathy for this rejection of properties, for reasons I will not discuss here, but the important point for present purposes is that such an ontology is quite incidental to the moral I am after. We could, if we like, stipulate instead that our sentence is true just if the predicate 'bald' is a member of the set of predicates true of the referent of 'Russell', thus dispensing with properties; we simply take the second-level extension of the name to be a set of linguistic items. Then again, we could also proceed as follows: take the extensions of each of the predicates true of Russell, assign these to the name, and formulate the truth condition thus: the extension of the predicate 'bald' should be a member of the set of extensions (themselves sets) assigned to the name. Suppose one of these extensions is the set of bald things; then the sentence would be true, since the predicate 'bald' has an extension that is identical to one of the extensions assigned to the name. Though this truth condition is somewhat less intuitive to grasp, it will be seen on reflection to be equivalent to the truth condition stated in terms of properties—for the simple reason that each property has its corresponding set of objects that instantiate it. So we can ask again: why not use this style of truth condition instead of the standard one? Actually, it is simpler in one sense to do it this way, since we are now dealing with a uniform ontology of sets at all points in the semantics. We need sets of objects under the Quinean dispensation anyway, so why not do the whole thing in terms of such sets?

It may also be complained that the second-level extension of a name is not known or grasped by the speaker—is not part of his understanding of the meaning of the sentence in question. That is true, since someone who understands 'Bertrand Russell' is not required to know all of Russell's properties; but it is equally true that the standard extension of a predicate is not known or grasped by the speaker either, since someone who understands 'bald' is not acquainted with all the things that are bald. Neither type of semantics meshes naturally with speakers' understanding. The type of semantics that works best in this regard is the type I am working towards defending—that in which we assign an object to the name and a property to the predicate. My point at present is that the standard approach enjoys no *advantage* in this respect over the contrived alternative I am constructing. *Both* approaches are faulty for much the same reasons.

Enthusiasts of Tarskian semantics might make the following point: the standard axioms for names and predicates differ in that the former assign denotations to names, while the latter specify satisfaction conditions simply by using the predicate (or its translation) in the metalanguage. Thus it is usual to have clauses like the following: '"Hesperus" denotes Hesperus' for names, and 'x satisfies "man" iff x is a man' for predicates. In the latter clause no entity is ascribed to the object-language term, while in the former this is the case. Doesn't this familiar asymmetry support the denotational view of names and undercut the parallel view of predicates? The answer to this is that we can easily invert the Tarskian treatment for names and predicates. Nothing stops us from writing: '"man" denotes the property of being a man', and then formulating truth conditions by saying, '"Socrates is a man" is true iff the denotation of "Socrates" has the property denoted by "man"', using the denotation axioms for name and predicate to derive the standard truth conditions. Once we have properties to play with we can write such things as: 'x satisfies "man" iff x has the property of being a man' and 'x has the property of being a man iff x is a man'. These conditions are all logically connected in the predictable way. There is nothing in Tarski to *preclude* a denotational approach to predicates, even though the standard axiom takes the familiar mention–use form.

But can we also give a non-referential disquotational axiom for names? The answer is that this is perfectly easy once we allow an ontology of properties or sets. Let us say that a property *P fulfils* an open sentence of the form '$a\_$' iff *Pa*, for some name 'a'; or a set X *completes* an open sentence '$a\_$' iff a is a member of X. For example, P fulfils 'Socrates_', where the blank takes properties as values (or takes predicates as substituends), iff Socrates has P; intuitively, a property fulfils a name 'a' just when a has that property. Here we have a treatment for names that assigns them no reference, officially speaking, and works by employing an ontology tailored for a predicate variable. It is exactly parallel to the usual method that employs an ontology of objects and interprets predicates by using them in conjunction with this ontology: instead of saying 'x satisfies "man" iff x is a man' we say 'P fulfils "Socrates" iff Socrates is P'; in both cases we just disquote the object-language term and attach it to the variable, thereby eliminating the semantic terms 'satisfies' and 'fulfils'. The Tarskian scheme by itself imposes very light constraints on the way we interpret names and predicates, so it cannot be invoked to justify the asymmetry in question. In point of getting the truth conditions right we can proceed either denotationally or disquotationally, depending on prior semantic convictions; just as we can get truth conditions right either by regular extensions for predicates or second-level extensions for names. Truth conditions by themselves underdetermine semantics.[5] My own view would be that we know antecedently that

---

[5] I am thus opposing the whole (recent) tradition of trying to work back from truth conditions to semantic analysis: getting truth conditions right radically underdetermines assignments of semantic values to terms. In particular, Tarskian constraints can be fulfilled in far too many ways. Our conception of the semantic properties of terms should dictate the assignment of truth conditions, not the other way about.

names denote objects and predicates denote properties, so we would want to write our Tarskian semantics so as to respect this fact. The illuminating and correct way to write an axiom for a predicate is then: ' "man" denotes the property of being a man', and we reach the disquotational truth condition by using the principle that something has the property of being a man iff that thing is a man. In any case, there is no impartial way to motivate the standard asymmetry deriving from Tarskian considerations.

Returning to first- and second-level extensions, we can note a further symmetry between them. The extension of a predicate typically varies over times and worlds, as new things become bald at later times or exhibit baldness in other worlds; but the same is true of the second-level extension of a name, since new properties will hold of the individual as time goes by or as different worlds are considered. If extensions must be such as to vary with these parameters, then our new extensions pass the test just as well as the old ones. Indeed, they pass it for the very same reason that standard extensions pass it, namely that objects change their properties with time and possibility. What does not vary in this way are the objects and properties that names and predicates are naturally taken to denote (they are rigid designators, temporally and modally, of these entities). The name 'Russell' invariably denotes Russell, while the predicate 'bald 'invariably denotes baldness.

Is there any reason to prefer the method of second-level extensions? Well, there is if you harbour a certain kind of metaphysical outlook about objects and properties, to the effect that objects are analysable as 'bundles of qualities'. On such a view, Russell just *is* the set of his properties, so the regular extension of the name is identical to its second-level extension as I am defining it. This metaphysical view makes properties ontologically basic, and so it is natural to formulate truth conditions accordingly: the property expressed by the predicate is among those that enter into the 'bundle' that constitutes the object denoted by the name. Of course, you can use this type of truth condition even if you don't subscribe to this sort of ontology, but if you do it will seem the natural and obvious way to go. So it is not as if second-level extensions have no conceivable motivation in general ontology. Someone like Russell himself, who disliked the notion of substance or continuant particular, might well favour the property-based truth condition. It is certainly there to be favoured.

It is easy enough to see that the new method can readily be extended to quantified sentences and other sorts of complex sentence. The variables now range over sets of properties and the truth conditions are generated in the same fashion as before: the set assigned to the variable (as its value under an assignment) contains the property expressed by the predicate. The second-level extensions do all the work that an orthodox domain of discourse can do. As far as I can see, no purely formal test distinguishes between the two sorts of approach; and this is not surprising in view of the power of the ontology of properties (the usual logical theorems will surely go through, *mutatis mutandis*).

If we were to adopt the new approach, we would come to see names and predicates in a very different light. Where now we are apt to find singularity in the name and plurality in the predicate, we would make the opposite dispensations under the revised framework. The predicate would have the job of picking out a unique property, thus asserting its singularity, while the name would be assigned a multiplicity of items—the many properties had by the object named—to which it dividedly refers. The name would be distinguished from the predicate by virtue of its inherent semantic plurality. In our chosen sentence, 'bald' would be the singular term, while 'Russell' would refer severally to the many properties had by that philosopher. Some might argue, on this basis, that we may as well dispense with the ordinary reference of the name altogether, rather as now some dispense with the property expressed by a predicate; after all, we don't *need* to mention it in stating truth conditions. We require only that the membership relation hold between the property expressed by the predicate and the set of properties assigned to the name; the bearer of the name drops out, semantically speaking.[6] (Of course, we need to regard Russell as more than the sum of his properties if we are to abandon him while embracing the set of his properties; just as we now regard a property as more than the sum of the objects that have it when we reject properties in favour of extensions. Both distinctions are of course correct; and the symmetry between them is instructive: objects are no more bundles of properties than properties are bundles of objects.) Some may even go further and announce that this gives the true ontological picture of the world, since semantics is the royal road to metaphysics: there are really just sets of properties, despite our usual assumptions about the existence of objects.

What is alarming here is how close to certain standard moves such arguments would be. The methodological point I am making is that there are far too many degrees of freedom at the semantic level of truth conditions to warrant such inferences and constructions. But I shall pursue the question of significance and morals after a brief metaphysical interlude.

The world has a certain interlocking structure, generated by the relation of instantiation. Take a single object, say my coffee cup: it instantiates a number of properties—it is blue, cylindrical, fragile, etc. These do not exhaust all the properties there are, obviously, since no object instantiates all properties. Now take all the objects that instantiate the aforementioned properties—all the blue things, all the cylindrical things, all the fragile things. We obtain a large explosion of objects from this simple operation, but still not all the objects there are. But now iterate the process and consider all the

---

[6] Can it be argued that we still need the bearer of the name to 'tie together' the various properties that compose its second-level extension? At an ontological level that seems true, but semantically the bearer still does not need to be cited in formulating truth conditions. And, significantly, the same can be said about the role of the property denoted by a predicate in 'tying together' the various objects that compose its extension. Again, there is no relevant asymmetry to justify the usual differential treatment of names and predicates.

properties possessed by all the objects in these classes—a colossal number! Now again take all the objects that instantiate this huge set of properties. And when you have done that you can repeat the procedure and get all the properties instantiated by that enormous class of objects. If you go on this way you may not exhaust all the objects and properties the universe contains, but you will certainly generate a very large totality out of just a few iterations—and all starting from a simple coffee cup. Perhaps some traditional metaphysicians will see in this a sign of the essential Oneness of creation—the inextricable organic Unity of Being. Be that as it may, what we do have is a branching structure that links objects and properties in a chain (as you will see if you draw a diagram of the steps involved): there is a fanning out of objects and properties as we trace the instantiation relation from the initial object out along its axes.

I find this chainlike structure rather beautiful in its simplicity and power, but I do not mention it solely for aesthetic reasons (not that these are insufficient reasons to mention something). I mention it because it is the fundamental ontological structure underlying the equivalence of truth conditions I have been indicating. Just as we can move from the property expressed by a predicate to the set of objects that instantiate it, so we can move from the object denoted by a name to the set of properties that object instantiates. We are simply travelling in opposite directions along the line of instantiation. No direction is any more legitimate than the other; both are written into the structure of the facts. In particular, there is nothing privileged, seen from the metaphysical standpoint just adumbrated, about choosing the extension of a predicate as the way to state truth conditions (or conceive of the structure of facts). The contrary method of forming second-level extensions simply proceeds in the opposite direction—by starting with the object and considering the properties it instantiates. We could just as well conceive of the structure of facts in that way: every fact consists in the membership of a property in some set of properties—instead of the membership of an object in some set of objects. Then, too, there is a third view, that facts consist in the instantiation of properties by objects—the view I favour. Thus we could depict facts in three different ways: $[x, \{x, y, z\}]$; $[P, \{P, Q, R\}]$; $[x, P]$. In the first, Quinean, way a singular fact is an ordered pair of an object and an extension, a set of objects; in the second way such a fact is an ordered pair of a property and a second-level extension, a set of properties (or we could do the whole thing with extensions and sets of them); in the third way a fact is simply an ordered pair of an object and a property. My point is that there is no particular reason to prefer the first of these to the second, and the third is really the natural view to adopt. When we appreciate what the underlying ontological structure is we can understand why both sorts of conception work—and how little reason there is to favour one over the other. At the risk of sounding airily metaphysical, we can say that every unity (object or property) has its corresponding plurality (set of properties or set of objects)—with these correspondences setting up a great chain of interlocking objects and properties stretching as far as the eye can see. The chain allows us to formulate our semantics in equivalent ways, by selecting the sets we fancy and assigning them to the various parts of speech in ways that preserve the requisite instantiation relations. How we do this is essentially arbitrary, unless some further constraints can be found and motivated. As it turns out, I don't think this is terribly difficult, but the necessary constraints rule out the standard Quinean approach, and hence determine a quite different semantic conception of the function of predicates. Extensions will no longer be in the picture.

One possible response to the availability of second-level extensions in formulating truth conditions is to declare deep semantic indeterminacy. A name indeterminately refers either to its bearer or to the set of properties possessed by its bearer; a predicate indeterminately refers either to the property it expresses or to the members of the set of objects that instantiate this property. There is simply nothing to choose between the standard approach and the alternative approach—no 'fact of the matter'. This would be quite a strong result, showing that there is nothing privileged about the standard approach and the conception of predicates it engenders; it really is arbitrary which way we choose to go. Names can be treated as having multiple reference to properties (or sets of extensions), just as well as predicates can be treated as having multiple reference to objects. Either approach delivers semantic values that work to fix truth conditions. Presumably this would not please Quine, despite his predilection for indeterminacy theses, since it undermines his general conception of what a predicate distinctively is.[7] But I can see how it might be tempting for some to draw such a conclusion.

However, I don't think we are forced to accept semantic indeterminacy here; there are other constraints that can be mobilized. The obvious, and familiar, move is to introduce epistemic considerations: roughly, we require that the speaker be *acquainted* with the semantic values that are invoked. This certainly rules out second-level extensions as the semantic value of names, since a speaker cannot be expected to know all the properties of the objects he refers to. But it also rules out regular extensions, since the speaker will not be acquainted with all the objects that make up the extensions of the predicates he understands. Such knowledge requires, intuitively, knowledge of facts, not merely semantic knowledge. What is not ruled out by this constraint is the simple view that I prefer: that names denote objects and predicates denote properties. When a predicate is understood what is known is precisely the identity of the property expressed by the predicate; just as understanding a name involves knowledge of the identity of its bearer.[8]

---

[7] So two Quinean sentiments are in tension: a penchant for semantic indeterminacy theses, and use of the singular–plural distinction to distinguish names from predicates. If what I have argued is correct, then that latter idea is nullified through indeterminacy considerations. In a way it is surprising that the kind of indeterminacy I am alluding to did not occur to Quine, given his ingenuity with contrived alternative semantic schemes.

[8] The kind of view of name understanding defended by Gareth Evans in *The Varieties of Reference*, in which individuating knowledge and causal relations are blended, could be extended to predicate understanding: we understand a predicate when we have individuating knowledge of the property it denotes, mediated by causal relations in which that property is involved. Or again, Russell's idea that understanding predicates involves acquaintance with universals mirrors the idea that understanding a name involves acquaintance with its bearer: see *The Problems of Philosophy*, ch. 5.

So we can construe what I have said so far as an argument along the following lines: if you don't accept this view, then you are forced to accept indeterminacy as between the standard approach and the second-level extension approach.

The simple view abandons extensions (of either sort) as semantically relevant and thereby relinquishes the idea that predicates are general terms in Quine's sense—predicates do not have multiple reference but rather are singular terms denoting properties. In effect, the 'true of' relation between predicates and objects is not semantically relevant. Of course, predicates are true of many things—but it is equally the case that objects satisfy many predicates: and we don't say that names of objects have plural reference simply on account of this. The underlying ontological structure always gives us a plurality for any unity, no matter from which direction we approach the instantiation relation.

The singular term view of predicates is confirmed by a well-known point, namely that predicates can be nominalized so as to give terms that feature in subject position—as with 'redness', 'mortality', 'baldness', etc. Here they clearly do not designate extensions, and so it is natural to assume semantic uniformity and take the corresponding predicates to designate properties when occurring in predicate position. Thus predicates are as much singular terms as their nominalizations are. Of course, that is not to say that they are *names*, in the sense of terms referring to particulars; the entities they purport uniquely to denote are properties or universals, not particulars. The singularity consists in their not denoting the members of a set of objects via the 'true of' relation; they do not 'divide their reference'. It is true that they are satisfied by many objects, but these objects are not components of their semantic value; just as a name refers to an object of which many properties hold without its semantic value being those many properties. A predicate refers to a property with many instances; a name refers to an object with many properties: that is all. The meaning of each category of term stops at its ordinary reference without reaching out further into the non-semantic world of property instantiation. Extensions of both kinds are fixed by the facts of the world, not by the meaning of the terms. They are extra-semantic items.

The asymmetry between names and predicates is not then a matter of singularity versus plurality of reference. Then what does it depend upon? Two things: grammatical position and the ontological type of the reference. Predicates occur in predicate *position*, ascribing properties to objects thereby. But they also denote a special class of entities—universals. It is not the *way* they refer that marks them off from names but *what* they refer to— and the sentential position they refer *from*. So it is not that no asymmetry can be found between 'Russell' and 'bald' in the sentence 'Russell was bald' once the idea of multiple reference is abandoned. We can account for the difference between subject and predicate without employing the singular–general distinction to do so.[9]

I would say that the idea of 'multiple reference' is a kind of oxymoron, once you really think about it. An ambiguous word like 'bank' or 'John' indeed has multiple reference, but an unambiguous word like 'red' has a unique reference.[10] We can always ask 'What does that word refer to?' and expect to be given a single answer— that is how the word 'refer' is used. The contortions of 'multiple reference' stem from a desire to avoid properties for (misplaced) ontological reasons; the notion has nothing otherwise to recommend it. It is certainly not the case that 'refers' is synonymous in English with 'true of'. Saying that 'bald' refers to the *set* of bald

[9] Frege, of course, accounted for the difference in terms of his notion of incompleteness: names of objects are complete expressions, names of concepts are incomplete expressions. He does not account for the difference between subject and predicate in terms of singular versus divided reference. I do not say his account is unproblematic; I am simply pointing out that rejecting Quine's account of the distinction does not leave us without resources of other kinds.

[10] Of course, there are also plural nouns like 'The brothers Grimm' which have multiple reference; but predicates like 'red' are not plurals, so there is no basis here for declaring them multiply referential. The idea of non-plural terms having multiple reference is what strikes me as oxymoronic.

people instead of to each bald individual severally is no help in restoring a measure of singularity, since the predicate is clearly not *true* of the set of bald men (no set is bald!). The predicate is supposed to be true of the *members* of its extension not of the extension itself. The extension of a predicate (a set) is not supposed to *be* the reference of the predicate; rather, the extension is made up of the many objects that are *each* referred to by the predicate. Quine's talk of division of reference would not be appropriate if the reference *were* the extension, since *that* object is as singular as you could wish. If the reference were literally the extension, then predicates *would* be singular terms by Quine's own lights, purporting uniquely to denote a single object, a set. We need to keep this distinction clear if we are to appreciate the force of maintaining that a predicate has plural reference: 'bald' refers severally to this man and that man and the other man, according to the Quinean conception, not undividedly to the set of bald men. My complaint then, once this point is clarified, is that this is not a natural use of the word 'refer', suggesting ambiguity where there ought to be univocity. Frege had it right in not assigning a semantic role to extensions for predicates: he assigned only a sense and a reference, where the reference is a function from objects to truth-values. A predicate does not for him refer to the objects of which it is true, but to the function that maps these objects onto the True and the False—something close to the notion of property in the intuitive sense. For Frege a predicate is a *name* (singular term) for this function, just as I am maintaining.[11] The Quinean idea of multiple reference is distinctly unFregean, a product of conflating the 'refers' relation with the 'true of' relation.

---

[11] Predicates are also rigid designators for me, as they cannot be if taken to designate their extensions, since these vary from world to world. I say that 'red' designates the property of redness in every possible world, as 'Bertrand Russell' designates Bertrand Russell in every possible world. Here again names and predicates are semantically analogous. See my 'Rigid Designation and Semantic Value'.

The general upshot is this: semantics should not employ the relation of set-membership between objects and extensions, but rather the relation of instantiation between objects and properties. A singular sentence is true when an object (or sequence of objects) instantiates some property, not when objects are members of certain sets. Set theory is therefore not the right format for stating semantic truths. Semantics is not about classes of objects unless it appears to be, as when we speak overtly of classes. In effect, Quine brought classes into semantics in order to oust properties, but he failed to see how far this could be pushed, notably in the direction of second-level extensions and their set-theoretic counterparts. The lesson, I suggest, is to return to the naive view of how predicates work: they function to ascribe properties to objects. This view of predicates is to the Quinean view what the usual view of names is to the second-level extension view—the natural precursor of monstrous offspring. Extensions are creatures of darkness; or at least lumbering monsters lost in the semantic wilderness.

4. NECESSITY

PHILOSOPHERS have been infatuated with the quantifier. Understandably so, since logicians showed the power and elegance of the predicate calculus. And it is always tempting to want to put shiny new tools to use. If we can translate some idiom of natural language into quantifier form we feel we know how it works; we feel we have tamed it. This is notably so for idioms of existence, as I discussed in Chapter 2: to make an existence statement is to make an existentially quantified statement; the word 'exists' disappears into its quantificational paraphrase. But I rejected such a view of existence, arguing that existence is best expressed as a first-order predicate. Similarly, it has been attractive to many to regard identity as definable quantificationally, by means of Leibniz's law: identity statements say that *every* property of x is also a property of y, and vice versa. Apparently singular statements thus get recast in quantificational form. I also rejected this view of identity, taking identity to be a primitive relation expressed by a two-place predicate. In the case of modal idioms we find a similar appeal to the quantifier, in the standard possible worlds semantics. To make a statement of necessity is to say that *all* worlds are thus and so; to make a statement of possibility is to say that *some* worlds are thus and so. Thus 'Socrates is necessarily a man' translates into 'in every world, Socrates is a man' and 'Socrates is possibly a wise man' translates into 'in some world, Socrates is a wise man'. Again, what look like singular sentences turn out to be general quantified sentences. In the case of identity and existence the corresponding idioms of natural language have the grammar of predicates, two-place and one-place respectively, while in the case of modality the idioms involved look adverbial or operator-like. But they all turn out to be quantificational in their underlying logical form. Not surprisingly, I shall also be rejecting this view of modality. The infatuation has gone on too long.

According to possible worlds semantics, we can replace any occurrence of a modal word with a suitable quantificational translation.[1] We take what looks superficially like an operator and interpret it by means of an existential or universal quantifier over 'worlds'—however exactly these entities are to be construed. Most of the debate has then been over what sorts of entities worlds are. But the objection I want to make to this is that such a translation is either circular or inadequate; specifically, we need to use the modal notion being translated in order to get the translation to come out right. The point is parallel to one of my arguments against the quantificational treatment of existence in Chapter 2, namely that the required notion of 'having instances' has existence built into it in an unanalysed form. So let us consider some proposition of the form 'possibly p': this is meant to go over into 'there is a world in which p' or 'for some world w, p in w'. Now the question I want to ask is: does the notion of 'world' here invoked include or exclude *impossible* worlds? Suppose it includes them. Then 'possibly p' will be true if 'p' holds in an impossible world. But that is clearly not the truth condition of 'possibly p': a proposition that is necessarily false is true in some *im*possible world! If I say 'possibly water is not H_2O' or 'possibly $2 + 2 = 5$' I speak falsely, but the embedded statements are true in some impossible world. So clearly the notion of 'world' must be taken to exclude impossible worlds. There seem to be two and only two ways in which this result can be ensured. First, we might say outright that 'possibly p' is equivalent to 'in some *possible* world, p' or 'for some w, w is possible and p in w'. But this now

---

[1] I will be limiting myself to this semantic claim in what follows; nothing I say here will bear on the use of an ontology of possible worlds for other purposes. The idea I will be criticizing is just the idea that modal expressions can be successfully paraphrased by means of a quantifier over worlds. Nor do any of my criticisms depend upon which specific ontology of worlds is adopted; they are intended to apply to all such semantic theories, from the most 'realist' to the most 'constructivist'.

contains an explicit use of the word 'possible', which we claimed to be reducing to a quantifier over worlds. In effect, we are now treating 'possibly' as a predicate of worlds, not as a quantifier over them. We are not *replacing* 'possibly' with a suitable quantifier but *using* it to limit the scope of the quantifier. So no analysis has been given of the force of the modal notion concerned. It might be thought that this is no problem, since we can always translate the offending occurrence of 'possibly' into quantifier form. So let's do that: 'w^* is a possible world' now becomes 'for some w, $w^* = w$', where 'w' is simply a variable over worlds and 'w^*' is a name of some particular world; we are saying that w^* is possible iff it is identical to some world w. But now the problem is whether w is a possible or an impossible world. If the latter, then the truth conditions are wrong; if the former, then we have a new occurrence of 'possible' that has not been analysed. And obviously it won't help to bring in a new variable over worlds to express that w is a possible world. The underlying point here is exceedingly simple: when we say that 'possibly p' is true we must be saying that 'p' is true in some *possible* world, but then we have the quantifier 'some world' *and* the word 'possible'; it is not that the latter has vanished into the former—on the contrary, the former *needs* the latter. What we really have in the standard variable 'w' is a restricted quantifier embedding the word 'possible', analogous to 'some man' (which clearly does not analyse the notion expressed by 'man'). We cannot allow the world variable 'w' to remain neutral between possibility and impossibility, on pain of making the truth conditions of modal sentences come out wrong. We have to mean *possible* world or else there will be no necessities and too many possibilities.

The second way to rule out the impossible worlds objection is to append to our truth condition the stipulation 'there are no impossible worlds'. Then we will be saying that 'possibly p' is true iff 'p' is true in some world w (not explicitly stipulated to be possible) *and* there are no impossible worlds in which 'p' might be true. There are two problems with this. First, we are again using a modal term that we have not analysed, viz. 'impossible'. We are taking 'impossible' to be a predicate of worlds and then saying that it has null extension. But the question is what this use of 'impossible' *means* for a possible worlds theorist for whom all modal terms are analysable as quantifiers. If we have to take it as primitive, why don't we do the same for modal idioms generally? The second problem is that the suggested truth condition fails to capture the force of the original proposition: it is no good saying that 'possibly *p*' is true iff '*p*' is true in some world, neutrally understood, and as a matter of fact there are no impossible worlds. That does not give us the idea that '*p*' is genuinely possible, since it leaves open the thought that '*p*' might hold in some impossible world; and that thought is not closed off by simply saying there are no such worlds. That just makes the proposition true by a kind of metaphysical accident; and it is no less accidental if we add 'and there *could* not be any impossible worlds', as well as introducing another unexplained modal term 'could'. No, the obvious point is that we must be meaning *possible* world when we say that 'possibly *p*' is true iff '*p*' is true in some world, or else this condition does not add up to what we need. We have to be *ruling out* the case in which '*p*' holds impossibly. Of course, we get the same kind of problem for 'necessarily': if we say that 'necessarily *p*' is true iff for all worlds *w*, '*p*' is true in *w*, we again have the question whether we are including impossible worlds. If we are, then the condition is too strong, because *no* necessary proposition is true even in the impossible worlds: even '2 + 2 = 4' is not true in the impossible world in which 2 + 2 = 5—but it is a necessary truth none the less.[2]

The point becomes even clearer if we switch from 'world' to 'state of affairs' or 'maximal state of affairs', since these terms wear

---

[2] This is assuming that in the impossible world in which 2 + 2 = 5 it is not *also* true that 2 + 2 = 4, so that this world is at least consistent. In any case, if there is a world in which it is not true that 2 + 2 = 4, then that proposition fails to hold in all worlds. Similarly, if there is an impossible world in which 2 + 2 = 5, then that proposition comes out possible under the stipulation that possibility is truth in *some* world, possible *or* impossible—which it plainly is not. Obviously, then, we must require that our world quantifier range only over *possible* worlds.

their neutrality on their sleeves. If we say that 'possibly p' is true iff 'p' is true in some state of affairs, we immediately invite the question what *kind* of state of affairs—are we including a state of affairs in which, say, water is not H_2O? We have to mean 'possible state of affairs', but then we are using that modal word again. We have become so accustomed to using 'world' as shorthand for 'possible world' that we don't notice that the notion we need must be construed this way: but then the problem is that we can't explain this occurrence of 'possible' by means of a quantificational paraphrase—there is always a residual occurrence of 'possible' that refuses to be translated into the 'for some w' quantifier. Ironically, it is the very use of 'possible' in the context 'possible world' that resists the possible worlds treatment. And notice that my point here is not that this treatment takes modality as primitive and that this is objectionable *per se*; my point is that the quantificational approach *claims* not to be taking modal words as primitive and yet in the end it has to. Just as the quantifier treatment of existence claims to be able to give an account of the notion of existence wherever it may occur, so the quantifier treatment of modality claims such coverage. But in both cases it is only a disguised use of the very notion in question that gives the would-be analysis an appearance of working. The locution 'has instances' must mean 'has *existent* instances' and the locution 'in some world' must mean 'in some *possible* world'. And the question is what these words mean in these occurrences, with the threat of regress that ensues.

The standard parallel with temporal discourse masks this problem for the quantificational treatment of modal terms. Suppose we say that 'occasionally p' is true iff for some time t, 'p' is true at t, and 'eternally p' is true iff for all times t, 'p' is true at t. Then certainly we are using the notion of a time here in a way we are not analysing; but that is no problem, since that notion is neutral with respect to the notions of 'occasionally' and 'eternally'—and the claim is not that we can always replace temporal locutions such as 'a time' by quantifiers. The trouble with the modal case is that we have the notion of impossibility to contend with, which forces us to reintroduce the locutions we are trying to paraphrase; there is no analogue for this in the temporal case. It is not as if we have to say 'for some *occasional* time *t*' in analysing 'occasionally *p*'. But we do have to say that 'possibly *p*' is true iff '*p*' is true in some possible world. The point about excluding impossible worlds simply makes vivid the need to speak of *possible* worlds in specifying modal truth conditions quantificationally; the supposedly neutral word 'world' cannot do the job. To be modally neutral in the use of 'world' simply leaves it open whether '*p*' is really possible.

This objection has nothing to do with the ontological status of possible worlds—what kind of entities they are, whether they are merely useful fictions, and so on. It applies no matter what view of possible worlds you choose to adopt. It is a strictly semantic objection concerning the project of translating all occurrences of modal words into quantifiers. And as far as I can see, it is consistent to hold that there are possible worlds in as strong a sense as you like and also accept my argument, so long as you don't go on to hold that modal terms are reducible to quantifiers over such worlds.[3] The semantic role of modal terms cannot be that of quantifiers, since such terms have to be taken as unanalysed even given the quantificational paraphrase. As so often in philosophy, the price of sufficiency is circularity.

What alternative might be offered? There seems little prospect of a straightforward predicate treatment of modal expressions, since this is not how they function in natural languages; they seem far more adverbial or operator-like. One approach that has been developed is that modal words function as predicate modifiers, like

---

[3] So David Lewis can keep his possible worlds, so far as my argument is concerned, just as long as he does not employ them as the domain for quantifiers intended to translate modal expressions: see his *On the Plurality of Worlds*. And there are clearly other uses to which an ontology of possible worlds may be put. For a further critical discussion of this ontology see my 'Modal Reality'.

'large'.[4] I think this approach is on the right lines, but I want to modify it in a small but crucial respect. Consider 'Socrates is necessarily a man'. On the predicate modifier theory, the logical form of this sentence is that the modal adverb operates on the predicate to produce another predicate, as with 'Socrates is a large man'. Modal words express functions from properties to properties: they take a non-modal property as argument, and they produce a modal property as value. Just as there is the property of being a man, so there is the property of being necessarily a man or contingently a man. Accordingly, we can say that our original sentence means something like 'Socrates has the property of necessarily having the property of being a man'. In addition to there being all the usual properties there are the modal properties that can be generated from them. Now I am a little suspicious of there being all these extra modal properties in addition to the usual ones—this seems like an extravagant way to handle the data—but I do not want to object to the predicate modifier treatment on that ground alone. My objections have more to do with explanatory adequacy. First, I believe there is another treatment that better captures the intuitions behind the predicate modifier treatment, which I will outline soon. Second, I don't think the predicate modifier treatment quite captures the intended force of the sentences it sets out

[4] See David Wiggins, 'The *De Re* "Must": A Note on the Logical Form of Essentialist Claims'. There are also operator approaches that treat modal expressions as one-place sentence operators, modelled upon the operators standardly employed in modal logic: see, for example, Christopher Peacocke, 'Necessity and Truth Theories'. I won't have much to say about this approach here, except to indicate later why I find the view I favour preferable. Let me just remark that there is nothing sacrosanct about the formulas of modal logic as a framework for a theory of the semantics of natural language, or as the basis of a good metaphysical account of modality. In fact, I think that modal logic, modelled as it is on the sentence operators of propositional logic, distorts our understanding of modal thinking. We should certainly not automatically suppose that the structures of modal logic properly represent the nature of modal thinking; they embody a theory like any other. Similarly, the standard treatment of 'not' as a sentence operator is itself a tendentious theory of the semantic functioning of 'not'; it is not the inviolable touchstone for the correctness of any other semantic proposal about negation. (I say all this to loosen the hold of any prejudices that might come naturally to someone steeped in the forms of classic propositional calculus.)

to analyse—and which the other view captures perfectly. So I am going to modify the predicate modifier treatment slightly, while sticking to its general spirit. The reason the predicate modifier treatment does not quite capture the force of a modal proposition like 'Socrates is necessarily a man' is this: it leaves open the *way* in which Socrates has the property predicated of him. What we are told is that Socrates has the property of being necessarily a man, where the copula here is modally neutral: that is, Socrates is said to have a modal property in a modally neutral fashion. So we can intelligibly ask whether Socrates has this modal property necessarily or contingently. But the original statement looks as if it already settles that question: Socrates has the property predicated of him in the mode of necessity.[5] But on the predicate modifier treatment the sentence says merely that Socrates neutrally has a certain (modal) property. As it were, the modality of the predication gets absorbed into the modality of what is predicated. But, intuitively, that is not how it is with the original sentence; it does not leave open the modality of the ascription. What this suggests is that 'necessarily' modifies what precedes it in our sample sentence and not what follows it—the copula 'is', not the predicate 'a man'. By modifying only the predicate the modality of the ascription is left open, but by modifying the copula the modality of the attribu-

---

[5] My point here is not that 'necessarily' implies the iterated 'necessarily necessarily'; it is that 'Socrates is necessarily a man' settles the question of the mode of instantiation of manhood in Socrates. The predicate modifier treatment limits the scope of the modal expression to the predicate term that it modifies and leaves the copula unaffected; whereas the approach I favour brings the copula into the scope of the modal expression, thus settling the question of mode of instantiation. On my approach, the predicate itself isn't strictly within the scope of the modal expression at all, any more than the name is; we could therefore as well write 'concerning Socrates and the property of being a man, the former necessarily has the latter'. Of course, if the predicate modifier position is interpreted to mean that the *predication*, including the copula, is what is modified, then the view is virtually indistinguishable from the copula modifier theory. What I am opposing is the idea that modal expressions modify *predicates*, i.e. property *terms*, as 'large' surely does. The lambda abstraction notation clearly suggests this latter type of view, since 'necessarily' here operates on a singular term (definite description) of a property, as in 'Nec$[(\lambda x)(\text{Man } x)]$': see Wiggins, 'The *De Re* "Must": A Note on the Logical Form of Essentialist Claims'.

tion is pinned down. If we indicate the scope of the modal modifier with a dash, then we can parse the sentence either as 'Socrates is necessarily-a-man' or as 'Socrates is-necessarily a man'. The first way of parsing it ascribes a modal property to Socrates but in a neutral way, while the second ascribes a non-modal property in a modally committed way. Thus the second parsing settles what the first leaves open, and hence corresponds more closely to the sense of the original. My proposal, then, is to develop the approach that settles what ought to be settled by any good paraphrase. This approach I shall call the copula modifier theory, as opposed to the predicate modifier theory.

I can sum up what I just argued by saying that in a modal sentence the copula is not modally neutral. And isn't this exactly the way we read such sentences? Don't they precisely say that a property is had in the mode of necessity or in the mode of contingency? We start by remarking that Socrates is a man and then, when our thoughts turn modal, we want to know whether this property inheres in Socrates in the necessary way or in the contingent way: *how* is he a man? What we are interested in is *mode of instantiation*. Modals are modes. To say that modal words modify the copula is the linguistic counterpart of the ontological doctrine that modality is a matter of the strength of the instantiation relation: does the object in question instantiate the predicated property only accidentally or is this a matter of logical or metaphysical necessity?[6] Thus, according to the copula modifier theory, we do not work with an ontology of modal properties; rather, we take the stock of non-modal properties and think of them as possessed in different modes. If you like, the instantiation relation is the only thing that gives rise to modal properties—the properties of being instantiated necessarily or contingently. There are two modes of instantiation and a fund of non-modal properties

---

[6] What of '*a* is possibly *F*', where this can be true even though the object doesn't actually have the property? In this case, obviously, we cannot be saying in what mode the object *has* the property, since it doesn't have it. Instead, we are saying that the object possibly instantiates the property, where again the modal expression modifies the copula, as in 'Socrates possibly-is a man'.

instantiated in these two modes, instead of there being a collection of specifically modal properties corresponding to the original non-modal properties. On this conception, modality is really not like 'large' and other predicate-modifying adjectives and adverbs. These expressions do not work by modifying the copula but by generating new properties. It is not that 'that is a red kayak' is tantamount to 'that reddishly instantiates being a kayak'; rather, the former means something like 'that has the property of being a red kayak'. Similarly for attributive adjectives like 'large': they don't tell us *how* something instantiates the property they modify; they tell us what (complex) property something has—as it might be, the property of being a *large* bee. The metaphysical picture here is that there are objects and their properties, including being a red kayak and a large bee, and then there is the modality with which these properties are possessed. The copula modifier theory is meant to answer to this picture.

There is clear linguistic support for the theory, since grammatically we often express modal claims precisely by modifying the copula. Thus we say 'Socrates *must* be a man' and 'Aristotle *could* be a farmer' and 'Plato *happens* to be a philosopher'. But there are no parallel constructions for 'large' and 'red' etc. When we convert 'is' to 'must' we incorporate the modality right into the copula grammatically, and this is the natural way to express modal claims outside of stilted philosophical usage. Just as we express tense by copula modification, as with 'was' and 'will be', so we express modality this way. The ease and naturalness with which we do this is evidence that modality is conceived as mode of instantiation. Incidentally, this also shows that the copula is not semantically redundant, since it exists in surface structure to be modified: given that there are modal words in the language, we would expect that predicative copulation would rise to the surface to serve as a lexical item to be modally qualified—and this is exactly what we find. We have the modally neutral copula 'is' and alongside it the modally committed copula words 'must', 'could', etc. Natural language is thus in favour of the copula modifier theory and the metaphysical picture it implements.

It might be objected that this account works smoothly enough for *de re* uses of modal words, but how does it handle *de dicto* uses? What about 'it is necessarily true that bachelors are unmarried males' and 'the statement that $2 + 2 = 4$ is necessary'? Surely in these sentences the modal word is not functioning to modify the copula in the *de re* style. My answer to this is that all such uses should be taken as modifying the copula as it attaches to the truth predicate. The canonical form of these uses is: 'the proposition that p is necessarily true'—consisting of a singular term for a proposition, the copula, the copula-modifying modal, and a predicate 'true' ascribed to the proposition denoted. The logical form of this is exactly the same as that of 'the teacher of Plato is necessarily a man'; the difference lies in the kind of entity denoted—individual or proposition—and the nature of the predicate. So on this account 'necessarily' works in exactly the same way in *de re* and *de dicto* occurrences. When we say of a proposition that it is necessary we are predicating truth of it in the mode of necessity; just as when we say of an individual that it is necessarily thus and so we are predicating a property of that individual in the mode of necessity. The difference is semantic ascent, with the accompanying need for the truth predicate. Truth is a property that can be possessed by propositions in the mode of necessity or contingency, just as regular properties can inhere in ordinary objects in these two modes. I think this is intuitively right and it unifies the *de re* and *de dicto* in a pleasing way. In a certain sense both uses come out as *de re*, since they serve to attribute properties to objects in different modes—it is just that in the case of *de dicto* necessity the object is a proposition and the property is truth. There is only one 'must', but it can govern different types of property; in all cases its logical function is copula modification. Thus we can say of the proposition that bachelors are unmarried males that it has the property of being true essentially—where this gets glossed as having the truth property in the mode of necessity.

It follows, of course, that such uses of modal words do not work as sentence operators. Superficially operator-like occurrences get translated into one or other of the two forms mentioned, most likely into the meta-propositional form with the attached truth predicate. Syntactically, we can still employ modal words as if they were sentence operators, functioning like negation in classical logic, but semantically they are copula modifiers always. I take it the needed translations are readily produced and entirely natural. Indeed, it is hard to know what it could mean to say that necessarily bachelors are unmarried males *except* that the corresponding proposition is necessarily true—and this lends itself directly to the copula modifier treatment. There is a clear sense, therefore, in which the standard formulas of modal logic, with their one-place sentence operators, are not a good representation of natural language modality—if the present account is on the right lines.[7] Not only are modal words not quantifiers over worlds; they are not operators on open and closed sentences—unless this is taken to be semantically equivalent to the copula modification translations I have proposed. We certainly should not simply assume that the sentence operator treatment of modality enshrined in modal logic is sacrosanct—that is a theory of natural language like any other. However, the two theories are clearly similar in spirit, at least as contrasted with the quantifier theory; I view the copula modifier theory as a more explicit and fine-grained expression of the intuitions that also encourage the sentence operator theory.

According to the view I am defending, instantiation comes in modes, the necessary mode or the contingent mode. It is always one or the other, though a predicative statement might be neutral about which it is. If I just say 'Socrates is a man' I do not commit myself to the mode of instantiation involved—the copula is modally neutral here—but the instantiation itself is always either necessary or con-

---

[7] Note that Quinean worries about opacity, quantification, and modal operators are sidestepped on the present approach, since modal expressions never generate intensional contexts—they never have scope over terms or predicates or sentences, even for so-called *de dicto* modality. Only the copula is governed by modal modifiers. Treating modality in terms of sentence operators obviously does court these objections, however.

tingent. The statement is well-formed and truth-evaluable, despite its modal neutrality. Thus we can say two things here: (*a*) it is not that 'is' is an incomplete symbol when it occurs unmodified, since the sentences in which it occurs have perfectly determinate truth conditions; but (*b*) instantiation itself comes in (at least) two forms, depending upon the modality involved. This may remind us of the topic of identity, where it has been held that '=' *is* an incomplete symbol and that identity itself (the relation) does have many forms. I rejected both of these doctrines about identity in Chapter 1, but it would not be incorrect to say that I hold a version of the latter doctrine for instantiation. Whereas, as Frege said, identity is given to us in such a specific way that various forms of it are not conceivable, it seems to me that instantiation is given to us in such an open-ended way that various forms of it *are* conceivable. If we are told that *x* instantiates *F*, we can always ask *how x* instantiates *F*—in what mode. The mode is, as it were, *internal* to the instantiation. Instantiation is a kind of determinable whose determinate forms are the modal modes. The linguistic counterpart of this is the fact that the copula admits modal modification in the form of 'must' and 'could be'. The identity sign admits of nothing corresponding to this.

I have suggested that modal words function as copula modifiers: but how does this work out in the semantics? What kind of semantics is appropriate for this general conception? More specifically, how do we contruct a Tarski-style semantics for this view? (I am not saying that the proposal stands or falls with the availability of such a semantics, but it is worth asking what the general form of a Tarskian semantics might be.) Without undertaking a rigorous treatment, I think it is clear enough what the general form of the account will look like. The basic shape of the axiom will be simply this:

x satisfies 'is necessarily *F*' iff *x* necessarily satisfies '*F*'.

And the axiom for 'possibly' will follow suit. Just as with the standard axioms in a truth theory, we simply disquote the object-language expression and then use it in the metalanguage in the same way it is used in the object-language, except that now it is combined with semantic vocabulary. Given the methods that have been developed to handle modal operators disquotationally, as well as predicate modifiers, there seems no difficulty of principle about extending these methods to the copula modifier account.[8] Basically, we use the disquoted modal words as copula modifiers in the metalanguage, combined with the semantic term 'satisfies', in order to interpret the object-language modal terms. This is really the easy part. The problems, if there are any, lie with the Tarskian paradigm—particularly, whether it is revealing enough about the idioms it seeks to interpret. But my aim is not to defend Tarskian semantics, only to show that the present theory can be slotted into this general framework.

Finally, what should be said about the iteration of modal locutions? Evidently it is well-formed to say such things as 'Socrates is necessarily necessarily a man' and 'Socrates is necessarily possibly a philosopher'—and indeed these sentence types exemplify the characteristic axioms of modal systems. I have said that modal expressions modify the copula, but is this true of *iterated* modal expressions? Well, if we take the view literally, then we would have to say that each iteration requires its own copula to modify—as in 'Socrates is necessarily is necessarily a man'. But this is patently ill-formed; so we had better not take the view quite so woodenly. The natural amendment, then, is simply that the modal word most proximate to the copula modifies it, while the iterated modal words modify the result of this modification—as in '*a* nec nec-is *F*'.[9] This is essentially the same conception that is standard for the sentence operator view of modal words, except now we are applying it to the copula modifier view. We regard the embedded modal words as within the scope of the outer modal words, so that changes of scope can induce changes of truth-value. So far as I can see the semantics is straightforward and the underlying conception sound. In fact, there is very little to choose, in the present respect, between

[8] See Peacocke, 'Necessity and Truth Theories'.
[9] If we view the initial 'necessarily' as forming a modal copula, as with 'must', then we can still say, simply, that all modal expressions modify the copula, since a new modal copula is formed by successive iterations of 'necessarily'.

this view and the predicate modifier view; both will handle iterated modalities in the same general way.

I now want to address some more metaphysical issues about modality, using the view just sketched as background. Since my aims in this book are primarily logical and semantic, I shall not pursue these broader questions at any length; but I think it is worth alluding to the implications for metaphysics and epistemology, so that we don't run away with the mistaken impression that the present topics are cut off from broader concerns. For the most part, I shall simply state, without much in the way of argument, what I think the broader implications are.

(i) According to the present view, modality belongs to a special ontological category: it consists neither in objects (unlike the possible worlds theory) nor in properties (unlike the idea of modal properties that goes with the predicate modifier view), but rather in items I have called *modes*. Intuitively, these modes are ways of binding objects to their properties, where the binding can be hard or soft, rigid or pliable. So an inventory of the 'furniture of the world' needs to include these *sui generis* items and not insist that they belong to antecedently recognized categories of entity. There are objects, properties, *and* modes in which objects have properties. Presumably, these modes are neither mental nor physical, but rather 'logical', for want of any better term. We might say they are topic-neutral, like causal relations, though this is not to say very much. They are logical in somewhat the way identity is logical— highly general, not specific to any particular category of objects. And of course they are the subject-matter of what we call modal logic. They are as logical as instantiation itself, the ontological counterpart to predication. They are also objective, in the sense that they do not depend upon minds for their existence (there were essential and accidental properties before human minds ever existed). Modes are objective, logical, real: they are what they are and not some other thing.[10]

[10] See my 'Modal Reality' for more on the metaphysics and epistemology of modality.

(ii) These modes give rise to epistemological perplexity. How do we *know* that a property is necessary or contingent? We can know that Socrates is a man by ordinary empirical means, but how do we come to know that he is *necessarily* a man? We certainly do not come to know this by sensory perception of the necessity in question. Such knowledge appears a priori if any knowledge is, and hence a problem for empiricist (and causal) epistemology.[11] There are many ways of responding to this problem, which I will not attempt to go into; what is clear is that modality is a prima-facie threat to the usual kind of naturalistic–causal–empiricist theory of knowledge. This is not, however, in itself a reason to doubt that modality is real; it simply locates a genuine gap in our understanding of human knowledge.

(iii) Do the modal modes have a hidden essence, in the way natural kinds like water do? I think it is clear that they do not—any more than identity and existence do. It is not that modal words pick out modalities by superficial marks, so that we might go on to *discover* what their underlying essence is. Modes are not natural kinds in this sense. They are *transparent* in the sense that their nature is given in the concepts we have of them. We might be able to go on and give a metaphysical account of their nature, but we cannot go on to give a scientific account of it: we are not going to discover the truth of 'necessity $= X$', for some empirical essence X, in the way we have discovered the truth of 'water $= H_2O$'. Modal concepts are not labels waiting for an empirical theory of their reference. This is generally the case for the logical concepts investigated in this book.

(iv) Modal truths seems to be supervenient on non-modal truths. If x and y are exactly alike in all non-modal respects, and x is necessarily F, then y is also necessarily F. For example, if x is necessarily human, and y is non-modally indistinguishable from x (say, a molecular duplicate with the same evolutionary origin),

---

[11] On the analogous problem in philosophy of mathematics see Paul Benacerraf, 'Mathematical Truth'; also my '*A Priori* and *A Posteriori* Knowledge'.

then *y* is also necessarily human. And this holds as much for *de dicto* modality as for *de re* modality, since the logical form and conceptual content of a proposition determine its modal status. Any proposition indistinguishable from 'bachelors are unmarried males' in non-modal respects is also a necessary truth. The modal is not reducible to the actual, but it is strongly dependent on it. In this respect, the modal resembles the moral, where we have a comparable supervenience of the evaluative on the descriptive. This means that there is no analogue in the case of the modal for the alleged possibilities of zombies and inverted spectrum in the case of the mental. That is, we cannot conceive of a non-modally specified duplicate *y* of a modally endowed object *x* that wholly lacks any modal properties, and we cannot conceive of such a duplicate that inverts the modal properties of its non-modal twin. For example: there could not be a duplicate of me with no essential properties at all, given that I have many such properties; and there could not be a duplicate of me that was (say) contingently human and necessarily a philosopher, given that I am actually necessarily human and contingently a philosopher. So there can be no 'conceivability argument' for something like 'modal dualism': here supervenience is written into our understanding of the concepts.[12] We reel at the thought that the modal might float free of the actual in these ways. And such supervenience is quite surprising when you reflect on it, since the modal is no mere restatement of the actual; modal truths are genuinely a new class of truths.

---

[12] There is thus no Kripke-style argument suggesting some sort of contingent link between modal and non-modal facts, unlike with the link between mental states and brain states: see *Naming and Necessity*, 144 ff. When God created the non-modal facts he thereby fixed the modal facts too. For example, when God created me a human being it was already settled that I be *necessarily* a human being; he could not make something of a certain natural kind and then be free to decide whether being of that kind is to be necessary or contingent. This is analogous to creating a situation with certain descriptive characteristics and asking about the moral characteristics of the situation: once God does the non-moral work he is not free to decide what the moral status of the situation is—any more than creating bachelors leaves him free to decide whether bachelors are unmarried or not. In these cases, supervenience seems assured a priori.

There is no possibility of reduction here, but the supervenience looks solid as a rock, scarcely in need of argument.

(v) From a causal point of view, modality is epiphenomenal. My weighing 146 lb. affects my causal powers in obvious ways, but whether I weigh 146 lb. necessarily or contingently makes no difference at all to my causal powers. Thus the modality cannot make any contribution to the explanatory force of my having that weight. And similarly for all my other properties. Only the actual can be causal.[13] In this respect, also, the modal resembles the moral. Anyone who took causal potential to be a test of reality would therefore have to declare modes unreal; better, I think, to abandon that test. It is an objective fact about me that I am necessarily human, but that fact makes no difference to my causal profile; so some objective facts are non-causal. The modal is not part of the causal order, though it is no worse off for that. And this is the underlying reason that modalities are not perceptible: they cannot cause themselves to be sensorily perceived.

(vi) Given all this, it is not surprising that modality is often suspected of being 'non-natural' and hence a potential candidate for 'elimination'. Without trying to argue the point here, my own position would be that modality is simply a counter-example to this type of naturalism, so that the project of elimination is unwarranted. The 'queer' is here, and we need to learn to live with it—even if we may not be able to bring ourselves to love it.[14] Modalities are part of what there is, problematic as they may be to certain philosophical perspectives.

[13] What about dispositions? Aren't they modally characterized and yet causally efficacious? This is a difficult question, but I am not intending to take a stand on it here; I am discussing so-called metaphysical necessity. My claim is that which of my properties is essential to me makes no difference to how the world works causally.

[14] For this general point of view, as applied particularly to ethics, see my *Ethics, Evil and Fiction*, chs. 1 and 2. My position here, as elsewhere, is that certain phenomena generate mysteries that we have no inkling how to solve—but that this is not a sufficient reason to deny their existence. It may be that the mystery stems simply from our conceptual and theoretical limitations: see my *Problems in Philosophy*, especially ch. 6.

5. TRUTH

DISQUOTATION is the essence of truth. This much is widely accepted.[1] It is less clear quite what this tells us about the concept of truth. My aim in this chapter is to articulate exactly what the disquotational insight implies, and does not imply, about what it is for a proposition to be true—what follows from it and what it reveals about the inner nature of truth. I think the disquotational property of truth has been widely misinterpreted, and that the correct interpretation of it shows truth to be a far more interesting concept than has been recognized. Specifically, I am concerned with the question of whether disquotationalism entails something deserving the label 'deflationism'. The view I shall defend, which I call *thick disquotationalism*, holds that there is something importantly wrong about the deflationary interpretation. Truth is a more robust property than deflationism allows, despite its disquotational essence.

Truth can be predicated of both linguistic items (sentences) and what they express (propositions). This difference will not concern me in what follows. For convenience and purity I will take truth to apply to intensional items like propositions or beliefs, so that the

---

[1] See Quine, *Philosophy of Logic*, 10 ff. As Quine famously writes: 'No sentence is true but reality makes it so. The sentence "Snow is white" is true, as Tarski has taught us, if and only if real snow is really white. The same can be said of the sentence "Der Schnee ist weiss"; language is not the point. In speaking of the truth of a given sentence there is only indirection; we do better simply to say the sentence and so speak not about language but about the world' (pp. 10–11). Many writers have given voice to the same sentiment: Frege, Wittgenstein, Tarski, Ramsey, Strawson, and others. For a useful collection of readings see Simon Blackburn and Keith Simmons, *Truth*. I will glide lightly over this large literature in this chapter, assuming that the reader is familiar with the general shape of it.

question of their semantic interpretation is irrelevant. Given this, 'disquotational' isn't quite the right word, since only words can be quoted or disquoted: 'dis-intensional' or 'dis-representational' might be more accurate. But I will stick with 'disquotational', warning that it must not be taken too literally. Using roman 'p' as the name of a proposition, then, we can express the disquotational property of truth in the following familiar way: 'p is true iff p', i.e. 'the proposition that p is true iff p'. Thus the truth predicate takes us from something referring to a proposition to something referring to what that proposition is about. Analogous general principles can be formulated for satisfaction and reference, as in: 'F is true of x iff Fx' and 'a refers to b iff $a=b$', where again the roman letters refer to concepts. My question, then, is exactly what the significance is of the truth—indeed the analytic truth—of these biconditionals: what do they tell us about truth, satisfaction, and reference? Focusing on truth, what is the concept of truth such that the disquotational principle holds of it? What is it about truth that makes disquotationalism true? But before I get to this, I want to make a few remarks about competing theories of truth and how they run afoul of the disquotational property of truth.

It can be quickly seen that the classic coherence and pragmatist theories of truth are committed to idealism of some sort by the disquotational character of truth, and idealism is not something one wants to be commited to just by virtue of one's analysis of the concept of truth.[2] This is because it is facts about beliefs or desires and actions that constitute truth according to these theories. Thus the coherence theory says that p is true iff the belief that p coheres with other beliefs, and the pragmatist theory says that p is true iff the belief that p leads to the satisfaction of desires or to successful

---

[2] I mean here, not the *nature* of truth, but the *meaning* of the word 'true'. Possibly, as some have argued, notably Michael Dummett, the nature of truth dictates an 'anti-realist' conception of the world. I am not intending to rule this out here (though I have criticized it elsewhere: see my *Knowledge and Reality*); my point here is that the ordinary sense of the word 'true' should not dictate an idealist philosophy—on pain of making idealism excessively easy to establish.

action. But now if we substitute in these biconditionals the disquoted sentence licensed by the disquotation principle we get the
result that facts about the *world* are constituted by beliefs and
desires. For example, we start by saying: 'the belief that snow falls
from the sky is true iff the belief that snow falls from the sky
coheres with one's other beliefs'. Then, by disquotation, we can
substitute to derive the following: 'snow falls from the sky iff the
belief that snow falls from the sky coheres with one's other beliefs'.
But this makes snow's falling from the sky consist in something
about one's beliefs—which is a form of idealism. Snow could
surely fall from the sky even if there were no beliefs in the world
to cohere with each other. So the biconditional cannot possibly
express an analytic truth, and it needs to if it is to claim to be a
definition of truth. Similarly for the pragmatist theory: it makes
snow's falling from the sky consist in a fact about human desires
and actions—which it does not. To say that snow falls from the sky
is *not*, failing idealism, to say that the corresponding belief coheres
with other beliefs or that it leads to desire satisfaction. There is
simply no analytic connection here.

That was the simple way to make the point, but it is open to a
natural reply: why not make the two theories conditional on the
existence of beliefs and desires? Thus we might say: 'given that
there is the belief that snow falls from the sky, that belief is true
iff it coheres with other beliefs', and similarly for the pragmatist
theory. Then we only get the result that, *given* the existence of an
appropriate belief, snow falls from the sky iff the belief that it does
coheres with other beliefs—and this does not commit us to idealism. No longer are we making the existence of the fact depend
upon the existence of the corresponding belief. But this only post-
pones the problem, because we are still saying that snow's falling
from the sky consists in the *coherence* of beliefs, or the *satisfaction* of
desires—and these are still mental facts. We are still committed to
supposing that snow cannot fall from the sky unless there is coherence among beliefs or satisfaction of desires—even though we
have made the disquotational biconditionals conditional on the

existence of beliefs and desires. Of course, proponents of these theories often had an idealist agenda; what I am saying is that this is built right into their theory of truth, once we take notice of disquotation. And we surely don't want idealism to follow directly from our definition of truth alone.[3]

The correspondence theory has a different kind of problem. Suppose we say, 'p is true iff p corresponds to the fact that *p*'. Then the question is why it is only the fact that *p* that p corresponds to, and not, say, the fact that not-*p*. For example, we naturally say, 'the proposition that snow falls from the sky corresponds to the fact that snow falls from the sky', taking the correspondence relation to relate that proposition to that fact and to that fact alone. But why not say that there is another correspondence relation that relates the proposition that snow does *not* fall from the sky to the fact that snow does fall from the sky? There surely is such a relation: it is the relation, not of truth-maker, but of falsity-maker. For any truth-making correspondence relation there is a falsity-making relation—the one that maps facts onto the negations of the propositions that they make true. So we *can* say that the proposition that snow does not fall from the sky corresponds to the fact that snow does fall from the sky—in the sense that there is a mapping from fact to proposition according to the making-false rule. Just as there is a function from facts to true propositions, so there is a function from facts to false propositions. But clearly that is not the correspondence relation we need when we affirm the correspondence theory of truth: we need the correspondence relation that takes us from propositions to their *truth*-makers, not their falsity-makers. So let us amend the theory as follows: 'p is true iff p corresponds to a fact that makes p true (not false)'. But of course now this is blatantly circular, since it uses the concept of truth on the right-hand side. The trouble is that the neutral notion of correspondence lets propositions and facts stand in the wrong kinds of

---

[3] In any case, my main point is that such theories of truth are committed to idealism, like it or not.

relations to serve the purposes of the correspondence theory; but if we tie the correspondence relation down in the right way we have to stipulate that it is the relation that holds when a fact makes a proposition *true*—which uses the concept of truth again. Correspondence has to be understood as truth-making correspondence or else it won't work. This explains the air of triviality that surrounds the correspondence theory, and hence its apparent undeniability: it implicitly builds the idea of truth into the notion of correspondence. Of course, if we read the correspondence theory as simply a windy way of asserting disquotationalism, then there is no problem; but if the notion of correspondence is to do real work then we cannot avoid the question *which* sort of correspondence—and it will have to be defined as the *truth*-making kind.[4] But there is no interest in a theory that says 'p is true iff p corresponds to the fact that p in such a way that that fact makes p *true*'. To put the point more generally: if we say that p is true iff pRx, for some relation R and entity x, then we need to know that R maps p onto the right x, since there are many relations that map propositions onto entities (e.g. the proposition that snow falls from the sky maps onto the fact that I am sitting at my desk, since there is the relation of being typed by a person sitting at a desk that relates that proposition to that fact). But what is it that selects the relation that intuitively constitutes the truth of the proposition in question? If we say it is the truth-making relation, we have a circle; but it is hard to see what else we can say to avoid this circle. Certainly the correspondence theorist owes us an answer to this question or else his theory is quite unexplanatory.

[4] Other types of theory have advertised themselves as correspondence theories—those that make use of a notion of representation, by way of either the reference of terms or the expression of states of affairs by whole sentences. I am not trying to dismiss *all* such theories by means of the argument given in the text; I am speaking only of correspondence theories that invoke a correspondence relation between sentences and facts in the way specified. I have no objection to invoking reference relations in giving truth conditions; nor am I objecting to theories that say such things as that a statement is true if and only if the world is as it is represented as being.

In the light of these problems, and many others I have not mentioned, but which are only too familiar, we do well to explore the prospects of the disquotational theory. Maybe registering the disquotationality of truth is all we need to say about truth to have a satisfactory account of its nature. This is a view that has been widely held and I am very sympathetic to it; but I think that the real import of the view has never been properly articulated—the task to which I now turn.

There has been a standing tendency to suppose that the right and left sides of 'p is true iff p' express the same proposition, that they say the same thing. This has fuelled a number of conceptions of truth that go by such names as 'the redundancy theory', 'the reassertion theory', 'the pseudo-property/predicate theory', 'the disappearance theory'. The thought behind these slogans is obvious: if 'p is true' and 'p' express the same proposition, then the former expresses no more than the latter, and the latter contains no predicate whatsoever that is applicable to propositions. The concept of truth gets swallowed up by the proposition to which we apply it. Thus we get the idea that to apply this concept to a proposition is simply to affirm the proposition, that 'true' is redundant, that it does not express a genuine property, that it disappears under analysis. To use the concept of truth is just an indirect way to say something you can say without it—something not about propositions but about what propositions are about. When I say that the proposition that snow falls from the sky is true I am simply saying something about snow, namely that it falls from the sky; the reference to a proposition cancels out, as does the impression of a special kind of property expressed by 'true'. Truth is simply a way to go from outside a proposition to inside it (so to speak)—a device of semantic descent: disquotation entails disappearance. My argument will be that this thesis is mistaken: disquotation does not entail disappearance. If we call the disappearance thesis 'thin disquotationalism', then my own position can be called 'thick disquotationalism': disquotation with a robust truth property.

What I primarily want to claim is that the left side expresses something logically stronger than the right side, so that they cannot be synonymous. The first reason for saying this is straightforward and I think uncontroversial, though its implications are sizeable (as I shall argue): the logical form and ontological commitments of the left are different from those of the right. The left side has the logical form 'Fa', a one-place predicate 'true' attached to a singular term for a proposition (or other truth-bearer); whereas the right—though it *may* have this logical form—typically does not. The left refers to a proposition and thus is ontologically committed to such, while the right makes no such reference and has no such commitment: it refers to snow and whiteness and suchlike things.[5] Therefore they cannot express the same proposition: for if propositions p and q have different logical forms and different ontological commitments, then they cannot be the same proposition. The plain fact is that the left side ascribes a property to something that the right does not; as I would put it, the left contains a predicate that denotes a property that the right does not contain, even implicitly. Thus the left has entailments that the right does not have; it is logically stronger in that it entails the right while entailing other propositions that the right does not entail. And this already shows that adding the truth predicate to a language expands the expressive power of that language; it increases the entailments of the language. As Tarski would put it, the

---

[5] What about formulating the disquotational biconditional with an operator-like truth concept, as in 'it is true that p iff p', where 'true' does not (allegedly) occur as a predicate at all? Two problems with this: (i) it is not clear that 'true' fails to be a predicate here, since 'that p' is naturally interpreted as a singular term; and (ii) we need a grammatical truth predicate to capture general statements about truth, as in 'everything the Pope says is true'. If we want to view instances of the truth schema as instances of such generalizations, as they seem to be, then we need a suitable predicate. Besides, the predicate version of the schema is clearly just as correct as the (putative) operator version.

metalanguage is always logically stronger than the (truth-free) object-language.[6]

Second, there seem to be cases in which the right side does not entail the left. Take any example of a proposition that suffers from truth-value gaps, according to your philosophical predilections—fictional propositions, counterfactuals, ethical propositions, vague propositions. Now it is not that I am myself particularly wedded to truth-value gaps for these types of propositions; my point is that the very concept of a proposition does not seem to imply that substituting it into the truth schema yields a truth.[7] Consider the sentence 'the proposition that Sherlock Holmes is a detective is true iff Sherlock Holmes is a detective'. Can't we quite comfortably affirm that Holmes is a detective without having to be committed to the claim that this proposition is *true*? For it to be straightforwardly true, 'Holmes' would have to refer to something real, but it does not, so the proposition cannot be true. There is nothing to *make* this proposition true, but it still seems to be a proposition; even if it cannot be properly asserted, it can at least occur as the antecedent of a conditional, so it can function propositionally. Or consider the view that 'the king of France is bald' is neither true nor false and yet expresses a proposition; if so, what propositions bearing the properties of truth or falsity does this proposition imply? It seems to imply nothing about the truth or falsity of itself; certainly it does not imply that it is true—if it did it would imply its own falsity, since it is *not* true (and not false either)! Propositions suffering from truth-value gaps cannot entail that they are true propositions, so they cannot entail the left side of a truth schema in which they occupy the right side. Most propositions are true or false, so this disparity does not show up in their case—we can

---

[6] Note that Paul Horwich, for one, unhesitatingly accepts this point about the logical form of the truth schema: see *Truth*, 38. Whether he sees that admitting this casts doubt on minimalism is less clear; witness his remark: 'it is not part of the minimalist conception to maintain that truth is not a property' (p. 38).

[7] Dummett makes this point about truth-value gaps and the disquotational schema in 'Truth'.

generally say 'if *p*, then p is true'. But this does not seem to be guaranteed by the very idea of a proposition, so it is not analytically the case that, for *all* propositions p, if *p*, then p is true. The notion of truth is more demanding than the mere notion of proposition—of what can be intelligibly *said*. We want to leave conceptual room for the idea of propositional speech acts that fail of truth and falsity. Calling a proposition true elevates it above merely uttering it. So there is no entailment from the right to the left of an arbitrary instance of the truth schema.[8]

Let us agree, then, that the left side is richer expressively than the right; and let us agree that 'true' really does express a property, just as much as any other meaningful predicate expresses a property. The truth predicate of a language is a genuine semantic predicate, ascribing the property of truth to what instantiates it. Now the point I want to insist upon is that this is *consistent* with the thesis that truth operates disquotationally. I want to put together these two claims—that truth is a robust property, and that it is disquotationally definable—and ask what conception of truth emerges. Here, then, without further ado, is the essence of the concept of truth: truth is a property whose application conditions can be stated without making reference to that property—moreover, it is the *only* property of which this can be said. Let us accordingly say that truth is a *self-effacing* property in the foregoing sense. The first part of the claim that truth is self-effacing is easy to grasp: the right side gives a necessary and sufficient condition for truth to apply to a proposition but it makes no reference whatever to the property of truth—the application conditions of 'true' are given without alluding to the property this predicate denotes in any way. We must be careful to understand this claim correctly: the

---

[8] There is, however, an entailment from the left to the right, which I take to be the heart of the disquotational analysis of truth. But since the entailment is only one way (though analytic in some sense) the schema cannot express an equivalence or synonymy, and hence cannot be used to underwrite a redundancy theory of truth. My overall position could be put by saying that the left-to-right entailment is what captures the essence of truth, once this is combined with the admission that the left is stronger than the right—that is what I mean by 'thick disquotationalism'.

claim is not the trivial one that the application conditions of 'true' can be given in other words or in other concepts. Obviously, we can give the application conditions of 'bachelor' in other words, like 'unmarried male', and obviously too we can give the application conditions of 'water' by using the concept H_2O. But in these cases we are still referring to the same *property* we started out with, though using other words to refer to that property. My point is *not* that 'true' can be non-circularly defined—for that is true of many concepts. It is that truth can be defined without even making *reference* to the property 'true' denotes—or using any predicate equivalent to it. That is what is special about the disquotation principle: it explains truth without referring to it in any way, under any description.[9] As we might put it, a shade paradoxically, truth applies to a proposition in virtue of something other than itself. I also claim, and will soon argue, that *only* truth is self-effacing in this sense, so that we can define truth as '*the* self-effacing property' and pick it out uniquely. More exactly, I will argue that no other property sustains disquotation: only truth allows the kind of semantic descent it warrants.

I am now in a position to spell out the essence of the disquotational nature of truth as I see it. There are two parts to this: First, truth is a property of a proposition from which one can deduce the fact stated by the proposition.[10] Second, it is the *only* such property.

---

[9] This is quite unlike the classic coherence, pragmatist, and correspondence theories, which all seek to analyse 'true' by means of some *predicate* deemed to be intensionally or extensionally equivalent to 'true'. That is why the right side of such analyses always contains a reference to the proposition mentioned on the left side. Seeing that this is the wrong *format* to explain truth is really the central insight of the disquotational conception: this conception differs in the *logical form* of its analysis, not just in the substance of it.

[10] This is shorthand for: truth is a property of a proposition from which one can deduce that the state of affairs represented by the proposition is a fact. Of course, not all propositions state facts, since not all are true. Rather, *if* a proposition is true, then the state of affairs it represents is a fact. No heavy ontology of facts is intended by this formula; it is just a convenient way to say that if p is true then one can deduce that *p*, for any proposition p. To say that one can infer from the truth of 'snow falls from the sky' that it is a fact that snow falls from the sky is just to say that from that premiss one can infer that snow falls from the sky. This is what I mean by talking of inferring facts from propositions with the aid of truth. I am merely locating the disquotational property of truth in an epistemic context.

Together: truth is that (unique) property of a proposition from which one can deduce the fact stated by the proposition. In other words, truth is the only property of a proposition which entails the fact that makes the proposition true. Propositions can have many properties—they can be believed, justified, denied; they can entail other propositions; they have constituent structure—but none of these properties entails the very fact stated by the proposition. They entail other facts, to be sure, but not the fact stated. This point is really quite self-evident: If you know that p is true you can thereby deduce that *p*. But if you merely know that p is believed or justified you cannot deduce that *p*—though you may be able to deduce some other proposition q. It is as if the property of truth enables you to look through the proposition right to the fact it states. In saying that truth is disquotational we are saying that it is reality-implying in this sense.[11] By knowing that truth applies to a proposition you come to know, not just facts about *propositions*, but facts about the *world*. And this is a remarkable thing once one takes the measure of it: who would have thought that there is a property propositions have that points beyond them to the extra-propositional facts? All the other properties of propositions stay at the level of propositions—whether they are believed or justified or entail other propositions or what elements make them up. But there is this one property that takes us outside propositions and down into the world beyond them. And this is directly related to the self-effacing character of truth: because its conditions of satisfaction make no reference to it, but only to objects and properties in the world, via the non-semantic right side of the truth schema, we can infer worldly facts from the application of 'true' to propositions. If the satisfaction conditions of this property were correctly stated by referring to it, then we would still be at the level of propositions; but because it is self-effacing in the way it is we can

---

[11] This is my gloss on Quine's 'No sentence is true but reality makes it so', quoted in n. 1. As he later remarks, 'By calling the sentence ["snow is white"] true, we call snow white' (*Philosophy of Logic*, 12).

move from its application to a proposition to a fact about the world. It is not that 'true' expresses no property, so that 'p is true' *means* '*p*'; rather, it expresses a genuine property that has the characteristic of being self-effacingly fact-implying. This is not then a trivial result of a synonymy, as it would be if we thought both sides of the schema said the same thing, but a substantive fact about a real property.[12]

How does it work with falsity? Falsity is not, strictly speaking, disquotational: we have the schema 'p is false iff not-*p*', and the right side is not a disquotation of the left, since it contains 'not' and p lacks this word. But we can easily modify the rule to accommodate this: if a proposition has the property of falsity, then you can deduce its negation—if you know that p is false, then you thereby know that not-*p*. Falsity is simply disquotation plus negation. When you know that a proposition has this property you can deduce the *opposite* fact to the one it states—so we have the same semantic descent and world-directedness for falsity too. And we can similarly assert that falsity is the *only* property of a proposition that licenses the inference to the negation of the fact it states (or purports to state).

Let us now consider some alleged counter-examples to the uniqueness claim. We should note that this claim is crucial if we are to have defined the notion of truth, since if truth is not the only disquotational property then this property does not individuate truth. (No one ever seems to concern themselves with establishing the uniqueness claim, being content to show that truth is disquotational—but this is clearly not enough if we are to have succeeded in fixing upon what distinguishes truth from all other concepts.) Consider then the concept of knowledge: we have it that if *x* knows that *p*, then *p*. So knowledge disquotes: you can infer the fact stated by a proposition from the property a proposi-

---

[12] Clearly, if the two sides were synonymous, then the inference would simply be an instance of 'p entails p'—we can infer a proposition from itself. I am saying, quite differently, that if we know that p is true we can infer that *p*, where premiss and conclusion are distinct propositions.

tion has of being known. Similarly for the property of following from something true, or the property of being believed by an infallible God. These are all distinct properties from truth, it may be said, but they all license the inference I am saying is distinctive of truth: so how can truth be uniquely disquotational? I take it the answer to this question is obvious: each of these properties includes or embeds the notion of truth, and it is this embedded truth element that is doing all the disquotational work. Knowledge, omniscience, and entailment-by-a-truth all imply that the proposition in question is true. So these are no more counter-examples to the uniqueness claim than the property of being both true *and* written in red ink is.[13]

Yet it does not seem self-evident that no other property *could* license disquotation. Take the property of being intelligible as applied to propositions. Certainly we cannot infer that grass is green from the fact that the proposition that grass is green is intelligible. But what about a proposition that says of itself that it is intelligible—the proposition expressed by the self-referential sentence 'the proposition expressed by this sentence is intelligible'? This proposition does have the property of intelligibility (just about!), and from its having that property we can infer that it is intelligible—but isn't that exactly what it says? So we can deduce that that proposition is intelligible, which is what it says, just from the fact that it has the property of intelligibility—we can therefore deduce the fact stated by the proposition from the property ascribed to the proposition. The proposition states that it has the property of intelligibility, and we can infer this fact from the knowledge that it has the property of intelligibility. Or consider the sentence 'this sentence is written in English'. That sentence has the property of being written in English, so we can trivially infer that it is written in English: but that is what the sentence says; so we

[13] Indeed, these alleged counter-examples are all analysable as conjunctions in which truth is one conjunct; truth is a necessary condition for each of the complex concepts in question.

can infer the fact it states from the knowledge that it has the property of being written in English. Or suppose I have a belief that is realized in my brain by state *S*, and suppose this belief has that very content—that it is realized in my brain by state *S*. Then the fact stated by the proposition I believe can be inferred from the property my belief has of being realized by state *S*. So here we have three cases in which there is a convergence between the property possessed by a proposition and the fact it states.

But I hope it is obvious that these contrived cases are extremely special and do not really threaten the claim I am making. My claim is that for *any* proposition truth licenses the inference in question; no matter which proposition you choose you can always make this move. But the properties just contrived are not such that for *any* proposition they permit the move—the move works only in these strange self-referential cases. It is not in *general* true that intelligibility, being-written-in-English, and being realized by a particular brain state allow one to infer the fact stated by the propositions or sentences with these properties. In the vast majority of cases such an inference would be lamentably off the mark.[14] So these are not counter-examples to the general claim I am making—that truth *always* permits the inference and nothing else has this power. Still, the putative counter-examples may serve to indicate why it is that my claim may not seem totally self-evident, since there is a kind of local violation of it in special cases of self-reference. The uniqueness claim is not trivial, though it is I think virtually unassailable. In fact, I think it is sufficiently obvious that no one (to my knowledge) has ever thought to defend it before—or even to formulate it explicitly. But it does need to be made explicit and evaluated, as I have done here, if we are to

[14] Obviously, establishing the truth of a proposition generally requires more than scrutinizing the proposition and employing logical reasoning; we have to investigate the subject-matter of the proposition. So the examples cited in the text are quite different from standard cases. Truth is reality-implying because knowledge of truth is reality-involving, one might say.

assure ourselves that we have captured the essence of what truth distinctively is.

It might help to bring out the role of the concept of truth if we try to imagine doing without it. Imagine being a member of a community of propositional beings who think and communicate but have no concept of truth. Someone says something to you and you register it, but you cannot apply the concept of truth to what is said. It seems, in these circumstances, as if you are in no position to form beliefs about the world as a result of what people say to you: all you know is that the speaker said that *p*, not that p is true. You cannot disquote on p and hence form beliefs about the world as a result of testimony, since you lack the device of disquotation that is the essence of truth. But now suppose you suddenly acquire the concept of truth, perhaps with the help of a friendly alien. All at once you can apply this concept to what people say and hence infer facts about the world. If you take what someone says to be true, then you can infer that *p*, for some *p*—you can acquire knowledge of facts. Of course, you can also come to know facts about the world directly without deploying the concept of truth, as when you simply see (say) that grass is green; in such cases there is no detour through other people's speech acts. But if you are to acquire knowledge of the world on the basis of testimony, then you need the truth concept. Truth thus comes into its own when we start using other people's beliefs to acquire knowledge of the world. This is the pragmatic side of the disquotational property of truth; it explains why we care about this property, what it does for us. Without the concept of truth we could not learn from others; no truth, no education.[15] Education is one long exercise in

[15] When I speak of 'learning' here I mean making a rational inference from belief-expressing speech acts to propositional knowledge of the world; I don't mean the kind of learning that results from imitation or conditioning or some such. We can imagine having a mechanism in our heads that causes us to form knowledge of the world as a mere causal upshot of hearing speech acts, where the concept of truth plays no cognitive role in this process; but this would not be a case of rational inference from speech act to knowledge. My claim is that this latter is what requires deployment of the concept of truth.

disquotation, using the teacher's beliefs to acquire knowledge of the world, this being mediated by the concept of truth. Without truth we would be condemned to be complete autodidacts.[16]

From this point of view, truth is essentially a device of inference. When I learn that a bird is yellow by seeing it I learn something about that bird, and what I might infer from this is incidental to acquiring that knowledge. But when I learn by testimony that a proposition is true the interest of this lies in what I can infer from this knowledge, namely the fact stated by the proposition. When I learn by testimony that the proposition that a certain bird is yellow is true what I learn is something I infer from this, namely that the said bird is yellow. I make a transition from proposition to world, and this transition is the whole point of the notion of truth. In saying that truth is a device of disquotation, then, we are also saying that it is a device of inference—inference to the disquoted form. It is not the mere fact that a proposition is true that is interesting; it is what can be inferred from this about how the world is that is important. Truth is essentially a method for deducing facts from propositions.

To bring out how special the inferential powers of truth are, let us formulate these powers abstractly. Suppose you are told that there is a certain property P such that when P applies to an object x it is logically implied that some other object y has some distinct property Q; and further that this property P is a non-relational monadic property. This would be like being told that the property of being yellow is such that when it holds of an object x it logically follows that some other object y is (say) square. That would

---

[16] Let me not be misunderstood: I don't mean autodidact in the sense of someone who is self-taught from books instead of from actual teachers; I mean the idea of acquiring all one's knowledge first-hand, from direct investigation of the world. Obviously, learning from books is an instance of education in the intended sense, and involves the usual process of disquotation: one reads the sentence, predicates truth of it, and then forms the corresponding belief about the world. You can pick up quite a lot of useful knowledge this way, and most of it has nothing to do with words and books at all. (I hope my reader has been engaged in the disquotational act steadily throughout this book.)

seem like a very remarkable claim: how can *this* object's being monadically *P* possibly imply that *that* object is monadically *Q*? Surely that is impossible: what has the condition of the one object got to do with the condition of the other, logically speaking? But this is precisely how truth works. From the fact that one object, say the proposition that a certain bird is yellow, has the property of truth we can deduce that another object, a particular bird, has the property of being yellow: we can jump between entities and properties using truth as our springboard. Moreover, we are moving from properties of abstract or linguistic entities to properties of concrete things: and that sounds like saying that the number 2's being even logically implies that a particular bird is yellow! But that is precisely what truth allows: from the fact that an abstract proposition has a (non-empirical) property, viz. truth, we can deduce that the world of concrete objects instantiates certain empirical properties. This should strike us as more remarkable than it does; we are so familiar with this property of truth that we fail to appreciate how anomalous it is. Truth is not just a device of disquotation; it is a device of ontological leapfrog—or rather, that is what disquotation really amounts to, properly understood. Truth forms a logical bridge between the world of propositions and the world of objects and properties; it enables us to travel from propositions to the objects and properties they are about.[17] No other concept can cross this ontological and deductive gap; truth is the only disquotational concept.

In the light of all this we can now state a 'definition' of the concept of truth, i.e. a condition that truth and only truth satisfies.

[17] Of course, reference is what mediates the link that takes us from proposition to fact. What truth does is enable us to move from a sentence to a fact by way of the reference of the terms in the sentence: if we know what 'snow' refers to and what 'white' refers to, then we can put this together with the knowledge that 'snow is white' is true in order to derive the conclusion that *snow* is *white*. Without reference we wouldn't know *which* fact to infer from a sentence's truth. And of course the involvement of reference here makes the leapfrogging power of truth perfectly unmysterious (though still remarkable).

Truth is to be defined as that property of a proposition that entails the fact (purportedly) stated by the proposition. This definition focuses on the disquotational aspect of truth and is intended to be a reformulation of that idea. But we can also define truth by employing the related notion of self-effacement introduced earlier: truth is to be defined as the self-effacing property, i.e. that unique property whose application conditions can be stated without reference to the property. Thus we can say 'p is true iff p has the self-effacing property' and offer this as a definition. These definitions do not compete with other definitions, say Tarski's; rather, they home in on certain features of truth, features that distinguish truth from other concepts. But the definitions themselves are far less important than grasping the unique (and remarkable) way that truth operates: it performs the miraculous feat of taking us from language and thought, on the one hand, to the world of objects and properties, on the other. No other concept has this power: truth is the adhesive that binds mind and world, to put it metaphorically and portentously. More soberly, when a belief has the property of truth (as opposed to any other property it might have), then the world is guaranteed to be a certain way, the way the belief represents it as being. If this remystifies the concept of truth, then so be it.

I shall now discuss the metaphysics of truth more directly. Again, I will be brief and dogmatic. The concept of truth seems simple in the following sense: it has no conceptual decomposition, and no empirical essence or nature.[18] We cannot analyse it into conceptual constituents, and we cannot expect to discover a hidden underlying empirical structure for it. Truth is primitive, in this sense (which is not to say that nothing illuminating can be said about the concept). In this respect, I would say it is like the other logical concepts investigated in this book: identity, existence, predication, necessity. These concepts form a conceptual bedrock; they stand, as it were,

---

[18] See Horwich, *Truth*, especially ch. 1.

underneath all our other concepts. They have no *analysis*.[19] But, despite the unanalysability of truth, it is possible to give a non-circular definition of the concept. This is peculiar: one would have thought that if a concept was simple and unanalysable then no account could be given of it in other terms. One would think, that is, that all we could say about 'true' is that it applies to a proposition iff that proposition *is true*. That is surely what one would say about 'blue' if one took this concept to be analogously primitive: 'blue' applies to an object iff that object *is blue*. But the peculiar thing about truth is that we *can* define it by means of the disquotation principle, even though it is primitive. Truth is a simple unanalysable property that can be defined: that is to say, non-circular necessary and sufficient conditions, of an analytically warranted kind, can be given for the instantiation of this property by a proposition. This is because truth is self-effacing: its application conditions can be given without referring to it under any description, and so its primitiveness does not stand in the way of providing these conditions. Truth is thus both definable and primitive (in the sense of having no conceptual decomposition and no underlying empirical nature). It is as if blueness could be the simple property it is and yet have application conditions given by reference to something quite other than blue objects. Put simply, the primitive property of truth applies to the proposition that snow falls from the sky in virtue of the fact that *snow* falls from the *sky*—and not in virtue of the proposition meeting some condition

[19] I mean this in the specific sense that these concepts have no sort of conceptual decomposition; this is not to say that we can have no *theory* of them, and indeed I have offered theories of all these concepts in this book. What I am denying is that these concepts can be *defined* in any illuminating non-circular way. Similar sentiments are expressed by Donald Davidson in 'The Folly of Trying to Define Truth', 320: 'Let me suggest a diagnosis of our aporia about truth. We are still under the spell of the Socratic idea that we must keep asking for the *essence* of an idea, a significant *analysis* in other terms, an answer to the question what *makes* this an act of piety, what *makes* this, or any, utterance, sentence, belief, or proposition true. We still fall for the freshman fallacy that demands that we *define* our terms as a prelude to saying anything further with or about them.'

that analyses (or simply reuses) the concept of truth. The predicate 'is true' holds in virtue of a condition not specified by the use of some (intensionally or extensionally) equivalent *predicate*. Yet it is still itself a genuine predicate standing for a real property—as much as 'blue' is. Therein lies the essential character of the truth concept, making truth an oddity in our conceptual scheme. Truth is really a very exotic property indeed, when viewed in the right light. And it is precisely the disquotational aspect of truth that lies behind this oddity. To call the disquotational view 'deflationary' therefore strikes me as wide of the mark: truth turns out to be *very* interesting in its workings, not the banality some people suppose.[20] Of course, it would be fair enough to use the term 'deflationary' if one held that 'p is true' says nothing different from—is synonymous with—'*p*', but we have seen that that is the wrong way to interpret the disquotational character of truth. Truth becomes interesting precisely when one accepts this principle and yet recognizes that 'p is true' says something stronger than merely '*p*'—in particular, that the former refers to a property the latter does not refer to. This is why I call the view I am defending thick disquotationalism, unlike the thin disquotationalism implied by the synonymy thesis. Truth is a substantial, robust property, as thick as any property, not the disappearing pseudo-property it is sometimes said to be. Or, putting the point in the formal mode, 'true' is as genuine a predicate as 'blue' or 'square'. What makes it unique is that it is a predicate that applies to an object (a proposition) in virtue of something other than a predicate of that object.

Does any version of supervenience hold for truth? I think it does: if you fix all the non-semantic facts, and you fix all the propositions, then you fix the application of the truth concept, analytically so. That is, if two possible worlds are exactly alike in the facts obtaining in them, and they contain the same propositions (which on reasonable assumptions they will), then exactly the same

---

[20] On the doctrine of deflationism see Anil Gupta, 'A Critique of Deflationism', and Hartry Field, 'Deflationist Views of Meaning and Content'.

propositions must be true and false in the two worlds. This is indeed a simple consequence of the disquotational biconditional, read from right to left. If snow falls from the sky in a world, and there exists the proposition that snow falls from the sky in that world, then that proposition must have the property of being true in that world. In short, the truths are supervenient on the facts. Here, supervenience is trivially assured. Yet it would be a mistake to say that truth is nothing over and above the facts on which it supervenes. Truth does not collapse into facts and propositions, since it is an irreducible property—though one whose instantiation is fixed by conditions that make no reference to it. Such supervenience may remind us of a familiar position with respect to moral goodness. G. E. Moore took goodness to be simple, unanalysable, and non-natural, but he also took it to supervene on the descriptive and natural.[21] I would say the same of the concept of truth, and I would adopt the same kind of realism about truth that Moore adopted for goodness. The truth property is a constituent of reality as much as blueness or electric charge or goodness is (though it is what we have been calling a logical property). It is a primitive constituent that nevertheless supervenes on facts that do not involve the notion of truth.[22] But there is a significant disanalogy with goodness, namely that there is no counterpart to the naturalistic fallacy for truth. We cannot deduce that something is good simply from information about its non-moral properties— there is always a logical gap here. There is always an 'open question' as to whether something is good, given that it has such-and-such descriptive properties. But nothing like this holds of truth with respect to its supervenience base: you *can* deduce that p is true given the information that *p* and the existence of p. There is no logical gap whatsoever here, thanks to the disquotational biconditional. So the irreducibility of truth does not result from a

---

[21] See *Principia Ethica*; also my *Ethics, Evil and Fiction*, chs. 1 and 2.
[22] Compare the modal and the actual, discussed in Ch. 4. I defend a similar view of colour as supervenient yet primitive in 'Another Look at Colour'.

non sequitur analogous to the naturalistic fallacy—there *is* no fallacy involved in inferring truth from fact. And yet the property of truth is not reducible to its supervenience base.

Where there is still an analogy with goodness (and the other concepts discussed in this book) is on the 'non-natural' status of truth. Truth is not a property that has causal powers or can be perceived by means of the senses; it is an object of intellectual cognition. It flouts naturalistic epistemology. It is 'queer'. But, as I remarked earlier, sometimes we just have to learn to live with the 'queer': denial and denigration are not sensible responses. What does seem clear, in the light of this non-naturalism, is that 'deflationism' is not remotely the right word for the kind of thick disquotationalism I have defended, if this is taken to imply that this view of truth is philosophically unproblematic or somehow 'tame'. If anything, my conception of truth deserves to be labelled *inflationary*. As I am conceiving it, truth raises many ontological and epistemological perplexities—but I do not regard this as an *objection* to the view I am defending. It is just the way things are.[23] Often the right view in philosophy is the one that identifies accurately just where the problems lie; evading real problems can never be the route to philosophical understanding.

This book has sided with what might be called 'logical realism', though that has not been the prime focus of my enquiries. Generally speaking, the concepts I have discussed have turned out to be more primitive and fundamental than has commonly been supposed. Reality has its logical properties too—basic, irreducible, real properties. This position raises many questions, ontological and epistemological, but I believe they are the right questions.

[23] I take the same kind of view of ethical properties in *Ethics, Evil and Fiction*, and the general metaphilosophy behind the view is set out in *Problems in Philosophy*. Ontological diminishment or evasion is not in general the right response to philosophical perplexity.

BIBLIOGRAPHY

BENACERRAF, PAUL, 'Mathematical Truth', in Paul Benacerraf and Hilary Putnam (eds.), *Philosophy of Mathematics*, 2nd edn. (Cambridge: Cambridge University Press, 1983), 403–20.

BLACKBURN, SIMON, AND SIMMONS, KEITH (eds.), *Truth* (Oxford: Oxford University Press, 1999).

DAVIDSON, DONALD, 'The Folly of Trying to Define Truth', in Blackburn and Simmons, *Truth*, 308–23.

DUMMETT, MICHAEL, *Frege: Philosophy of Language* (London: Duckworth, 1973).

—— 'Truth', in P. F. Strawson (ed.), *Philosophical Logic* (Oxford: Oxford University Press, 1967), 49–69.

EVANS, GARETH, *The Varieties of Reference* (Oxford: Clarendon Press, 1982).

FIELD, HARTRY, 'Deflationist Views of Meaning and Content', in Blackburn and Simmons, *Truth*, 351–91.

FREGE, GOTTLOB, *Basic Laws of Arithmetic*, trans. Montgomery Furth, 2 vols. (Berkeley and Los Angeles: University of California Press, 1967).

—— *Foundations of Arithmetic*, trans. J. L. Austin (Oxford: Basil Blackwell, 1950).

—— 'On Sense and Reference', in P. Geach and M. Black (eds.), *Translations from the Philosophical Writings of Gottlob Frege* (Oxford: Basil Blackwell, 1980).

GEACH, P. T., *Logic Matters* (Oxford: Basil Blackwell, 1972).

GUPTA, ANIL, 'A Critique of Deflationism', in Blackburn and Simmons, *Truth*, 282–308.

HORWICH, PAUL, *Truth* (Oxford: Basil Blackwell, 1990).

KRIPKE, SAUL, 'Identity and Necessity', in M. Munitz (ed.), *Identity and Individuation* (New York: New York University Press, 1971), 135–64.

—— *Naming and Necessity* (Cambridge, Mass.: Harvard University Press, 1972).

LEWIS, DAVID, *On the Plurality of Worlds* (Oxford: Basil Blackwell, 1986).

McGINN, COLIN, 'Another Look at Colour', in McGinn, *Knowledge and Reality*, 298–313.

McGINN, COLIN, '*A Priori* and *A Posteriori* Knowledge', in McGinn, *Knowledge and Reality*, 36–49.

—— *Ethics, Evil and Fiction* (Oxford: Clarendon Press, 1997).

—— *Knowledge and Reality* (Oxford: Oxford University Press, 1999).

—— 'Modal Reality', in McGinn, *Knowledge and Reality*, 65–110.

—— *Problems in Philosophy* (Oxford: Basil Blackwell, 1993).

—— 'Rigid Designation and Semantic Value', *Philosophical Quarterly*, 32/127 (Apr. 1982), 97–115.

MOORE, G. E., *Principia Ethica*, rev. edn. (Cambridge: Cambridge University Press, 1993).

PEACOCKE, CHRISTOPHER, 'Necessity and Truth Theories', *Journal of Philosophical Logic*, 7 (1978), 473–500.

PEARS, DAVID, 'Is Existence a Predicate?', in P. F. Strawson (ed.), *Philosophical Logic* (Oxford: Oxford University Press, 1967), 97–102.

PERRY, JOHN, 'The Problem of the Essential Indexical', *Nous*, 13 (1979), 3–21.

—— 'The Same F', *Philosophical Review*, 79 (1970), 181–200.

QUINE, W. V., *Philosophy of Logic*, 2nd edn. (Cambridge, Mass.: Harvard University Press, 1986).

—— *Word and Object* (Cambridge, Mass.: MIT Press, 1960).

RUSSELL, BERTRAND, 'The Philosophy of Logical Atomism', in R. C. Marsh (ed.), *Logic and Knowledge* (London: George Allen & Unwin, 1956).

—— *The Problems of Philosophy* (Oxford: Oxford University Press, 1912).

WIGGINS, DAVID, 'The *De Re* "Must": A Note on the Logical Form of Essentialist Claims', in Gareth Evans and John McDowell (eds.), *Truth and Meaning* (Oxford: Clarendon Press, 1976).

—— *Sameness and Substance* (Cambridge, Mass.: Harvard University Press, 1980).

WITTGENSTEIN, LUDWIG, *Tractatus Logico-Philosophicus*, trans. David Pears and Brian McGuinness (London: Routledge & Kegan Paul, 1961).

INDEX